What can I do with... no degree?

What can I do with...
no degree?

3rd edition
Margaret McAlpine

What can I do with...no degree?

This third edition published in 2008 by Trotman Publishing, a division of Crimson Publishing Ltd., Westminster House, Kew Road, Richmond, Surrey TW9 2ND

© Trotman Publishing 2008

First edition published by Trotman & Co Ltd in 2002 Second edition published by Trotman & Co Ltd in 2004

Author: Margaret McAlpine
Third edition revised by Monica Brand

British Library Cataloguing in Publication Data
A catalogue record for this book is available from the British Library

ISBN 978-1-84455-167-5

Typeset by Newgen Imaging Systems Pvt Ltd.

Printed and bound in Great Britain by The Cromwell Press, Trowbridge, Wiltshire

Contents

About the Author

Margaret McAlpine taught for a number of years in schools and colleges in the Midlands and East Anglia before becoming a journalist. Today she writes for a number of publications and has a particular interest in writing careers material for young people. She has three grown-up children and lives with her husband in Suffolk.

Introduction

YOU DON'T NEED A DEGREE TO GET ON IN LIFE!

There are many interesting jobs with excellent prospects open to people who have not been to university. A quick glance at the City & Guilds' UK vocational rich list reveals that very few millionaires who are household names hold a degree and yet they've reached the top of their profession; think of Jamie Oliver, David Beckham...

Some people need or want to start earning money as soon as possible. Others haven't enjoyed school particularly and are ready for a change. It may be that a Saturday job or a hobby has fired interest in a particular kind of work. Whatever the reason, each year thousands of young people make a positive decision to find a job – one which offers training and good prospects for the future.

Going to university can be an expensive choice. The National Union of Students calculates the average cost of a three-year degree course today is almost £24,000. This includes annual university tuition fees of £3,145 (which rise annually, with inflation) and a student loan to cover living expenses of about £4,625 each year. Of course, most students have part-time jobs to help reduce their debts – but, despite non-repayable grants introduced for some in 2008, graduates will spend a number of years paying back loans.

CHOOSING WHAT TO DO

For some jobs, such as medicine, veterinary science, social work and physiotherapy, you need a degree. There are other jobs where it is a strong advantage to have a degree. For example, non-graduates do become solicitors or town planners but the training takes a long time and many trainees give up on the way.

The first step towards deciding what to do after leaving school – even, when to leave school – is to consider the type of job you want: work in an office, studio, laboratory, outdoors, with children, with animals, with technology? Do you want a chance to travel or do you want to work close to home?

A good place to do this research is a Connexions or careers office. Here, you can access interactive programs designed to match your particular qualification level, skills and interests to possible jobs. Also, if you need further help, there are qualified careers advisers close at hand.

LEARNING THROUGH DOING

Some people understand and learn tasks best through *doing* rather than through learning the theory. They flourish once they leave the classroom and are able to concentrate on developing practical skills. Such people often surprise themselves (and others) once they find themselves in a work situation that suits them!

Whether you enjoy school or not, it is definitely worthwhile gaining the best results possible at GCSE level. For some people this could mean A*s, for others, much lower grades. Whether you gain As or Ds, achieving a personal best indicates to future employers that you can retain and use information and would make a reliable member of their workforce. Also, success gives you a real sense of achievement!

New 14–19 specialised Diploma courses start in schools and colleges in September 2008. The Diplomas combine the development of practical skills with technical understanding and a background of theoretical knowledge. They will be offered at Levels 1 (Foundation), 2 (GCSE equivalent) and 3 (Advanced) and the first Diplomas are available in Construction, Creative and Media, Engineering, Health and Social Care, and ICT.

If you're taking a post-16 Level 3 course – A-levels, Highers or a BTEC National – but feel it's not for you, you may be tempted to give up formal learning and find a job. In this situation, the best advice is do nothing in haste – first, seek professional careers advice. After just a few weeks of a new course, most people feel overwhelmed, but coping strategies usually kick in.

Give yourself time when making important decisions about your future.

FINDING A JOB WITH A FUTURE

Today's employers look for reliable, keen employees who have some qualifications.

Learning as you earn can often be the best option as it shows a disciplined approach towards gaining skills specific to your chosen work area. Also, it can indicate an awareness of opportunities beyond your present job and a desire to progress!

Working and going to college, or doing an Apprenticeship, ensures that you gain qualifications while earning some money. This means that you will get ahead and be successful in the world of work.

APPRENTICESHIPS

The most usual form of training for young people today is an Apprenticeship leading to National Vocational Qualifications (NVQs) or Scottish Vocational Qualifications (SVQs). These are work-based, practical qualifications that accredit individuals for doing a job well. (In the work-place, NVQs/SVQs are available at Levels 1–5.) All Apprenticeships include training in Key Skills (Core Skills in Scotland) in areas such as communication, numeracy, information technology, teamworking and problem solving. These are all skills that help people cope successfully in work.

An Apprenticeship is a chance to have a job, be paid and gain qualifications, all at the same time. The training is suitable for every young person aged 14 to 24+ with the ability to gain a qualification while working. The training leads to widening opportunities for promotion. A current trend in job creation is thousands of new posts for junior managers and technicians; these are the kinds of jobs filled by completing Apprentices.

Employers and Sector Skills Councils influence the design of Apprenticeships, so the training closely matches industries' skills needs. Apprenticeships are now available in more than 80 vocational areas.

Apprenticeship training forms a vocational 'ladder' of opportunities. There are Young Apprenticeships for well-motivated pupils aged 14+. These lead on to full Apprenticeships, which cover work-based training and learning to achieve a Technical Certificate and NVQ/SVQ at Level 2. You can progress from an Apprenticeship to an Advanced Apprenticeship which delivers higher-level programmes to NVQ/SVQ Level 3 and can give entry to a Foundation degree – a Level 4 qualification. In Scotland, Apprenticeships are called Scottish Modern Apprenticeships and in Wales they are called Modern Apprenticeships. For information about Apprenticeships in your area, contact your local Connexions/careers centre.

The usual route into Apprenticeship is by getting a job with an employer who offers the training. The job and the training are linked. Some employers require GCSEs or Scottish Standard grades at certain levels, while others select Apprentices through interviews and school records. Most Apprenticeships last three to four years, but individuals are able to work at their own pace and can take a shorter or longer time, as required.

Not ready for Apprenticeship and the workplace? The e-2-e Entry to Employment programme is a pre-Apprenticeship route into the programme.

What if you are over 25? Apprenticeship for Adults has removed the age cap to achieving Apprenticeship qualifications. Ask for more information in your local Connexions/careers office.

Find out more:

- www.apprenticeships.org
- www.scottish-enterprise.com/modern-apprenticeships
- www.elwa.ac.uk for Modern Apprenticeship in Wales
- www.connexions-direct.com/work for information on e-2-e

WARNING!

This book is only the beginning. It covers just some of the enormous number of jobs on offer. If it doesn't include your particular area of interest, don't assume that work and training are not available. Ask questions, try your school careers library, visit the local Connexions or careers office – you'll be surprised at the opportunities out there for somebody like you! Good luck...

1 Administration, Business and Financial Services

ADMINISTRATION

However large or small an operation, administrative work has to be done efficiently or the organisation will quickly collapse into chaos. Personal assistants are taking on more central roles and carrying wider responsibilities that can include project management and middle management-level tasks. Their pay is rising, accordingly.

Job titles vary, for example you might hear administrative assistant, secretary, personal assistant or administration/office manager, but the work has certain tasks in common, such as replying to correspondence and emails, filing paperwork, organising meetings, writing agendas, minutes and reports, handling phone calls sometimes and acting as receptionist. Jobs can include tasks requiring skill with numbers.

Job opportunities

There are administrative openings in almost every type of organisation: hotels, schools, central and local government offices, banks and building societies, in manufacturing and production, shops, hospitals, travel agencies, commercial businesses, financial service companies, news agencies and television companies.

The Civil Service, which is made up of separate departments and executive agencies, offers an enormous number of administrative jobs.

If you have Maths at GCSE/Scottish Standard grade at A–C/1–3 or A-level/Scottish Higher Maths or Accountancy, there are hundreds of advertisements for jobs with a financial focus within local government departments, printers, manufacturing and construction firms seeking, for example, bookkeepers, administrative clerks, cashiers or junior clerks in payroll and accounts departments.

A number of secretaries choose to specialise in a particular line of work, for example, becoming farm secretaries, medical or legal secretaries.

Skills and qualities needed

A good standard of written and spoken English is vital; so is an eye for detail, a good memory and a flair for organisation. Tact and discretion are important, as is being a team-player. Basic keyboard and word-processing skills are required for all jobs. Some employers require evidence of a strong ability with numbers. Today, with word-recognition software, few employers ask for shorthand skills.

Salaries

Rates of pay vary enormously, from around £10,000 per year at entry, up to £20,000+ for those with qualifications, experience and additional responsibilities. London positions carry the best salaries; experienced bilingual secretaries can earn over £30,000 annually.

Ways into work

Apprenticeships and Advanced Apprenticeships in Business Administration offer opportunities to gain an NVQ/SVQ Level 2 or 3.

If you are looking for a career in administration, you can acquire basic qualifications in IT, perhaps while you're at school, then aim for a job in a company that offers training. With motivation and the right experience, progression pathways for administrators can be impressive. Alternatively, you could take a secretarial course for which entry requirements are likely to be GCSE/Scottish Standard grades A–C/1–3 or equivalent qualifications. Courses usually last one or two years and can lead to qualifications such as:

- City & Guilds Pitman Qualification Diploma
- OCR Diploma and Higher Diploma in Administrative and Secretarial Procedures

- London Chamber of Commerce and Industry Examination Board (LCCIEB) Executive Secretary and Private Secretary's Diplomas.

These qualifications can be combined with a two-year Business Studies A-level or a BTEC National Certificate in Business and Finance. Ambitious administrative officers can continue to a Higher National Certificate (HNC) in the same area of study.

The Civil Service

Over half a million people work in departments of the Civil Service. Administrative assistants are junior clerical staff. Each department and agency specifies the basic qualifications they require; these vary, depending on the type and level of the job.

It is also possible to go in at junior management level. Minimum entry requirements are likely to be five GCSE/Scottish Standard grades plus a good standard achieved in A-levels/Scottish Higher grades.

Specialist secretarial jobs

Medical secretary

The Association of Medical Secretaries, Practice Managers, Administrators and Receptionists (AMSPAR) validates qualifications for medical secretaries. Many state and privately run colleges offer full- or part-time courses, lasting from one to two years, leading to the AMSPAR Diploma. Entry qualifications are four GCSEs/Scottish Standard grades A–C/1–3, plus a good standard of written and spoken English.

Legal secretary

People with general secretarial qualifications often work in legal practices. However, there are specialist legal secretarial qualifications and many employers offer distance learning and part-time training opportunities to their staff.

A number of legal secretarial courses are available at colleges across the country. They include:

- Institute of Legal Executives – Legal Secretaries' Certificate and Diploma (based on NVQs/SVQs)
- Institute of Paralegal Training – Legal Secretaries' Certificate and Diploma.

Entry requirements vary, but are likely to be a minimum of GCSE/Scottish Standard grades A–C/1–3.

Farm secretary

Rather than specialist qualifications, many farm secretaries possess knowledge of agriculture and general secretarial skills. However, training is available through part-time and correspondence courses and some agricultural colleges offer a full-time specialist course, such as that of the Institute of Agricultural Secretaries and Administrators leading to the National Certificate for Farm Secretaries.

Entry requirements are three GCSEs/Scottish Standard grades A–C/1–3, a good standard of English and maths and some ability in information technology. Applicants must be over 17 years old.

Finding a job

Information on Apprenticeships is available from your local Connexions/careers service, which can also offer advice on careers in business and holds local job opportunities for those aged 16–19.

Job vacancies are frequently advertised in local newspapers/ websites.

For information on college courses, see individual prospectuses.

CASE STUDY

Caroline Moyses – Medical Legal Secretary

Caroline's early ambition was to be a nurse. She studied sciences at college after leaving school, but then took the Association of

Medical Secretaries, Practice Managers, Administrators and Receptionists (AMSPAR) Certificate in General Practice Reception. She found the course extremely interesting and says,

'I was in a good position because I'd studied science and gained keyboard skills at school, which meant I completed the course quite quickly. As well as covering secretarial and admin subjects, we also studied medical terminology so we could understand some of the technical terms we would come across in our future work.

'We evaluated health promotion activities such as projects to persuade people to stop smoking, eat a balanced diet and exercise regularly. We also learned about patient care and ways of dealing with people who are agitated or upset.

'After finishing my course I took a three-month job with a medical practice and I'm still there!

'As medical legal secretary I deal with patient referrals, sending hospitals the details of patients needing to see consultants and undergo investigations. The legal part of my work is largely working on insurance claims dealt with by the practice. Recent years have seen a big rise in the number of legal cases brought by people whose injury or illness may have been caused by negligence or some other reason. Such claims involve medical examinations and reports by doctors and I deal with the administrative side of this work.

'When the practice secretary is away, I chase up appointments and carry out Health Authority work, transferring medical records when patients move out of the area.

'I try to keep up with developments and recently gained the British Computer Society's European Computer Driving Licence. Next I'm working towards the Advanced Diploma for Medical Secretaries Level 3. Whatever the job, keeping up with new training and qualifications is vital.'

FINANCIAL SERVICES

This industry is an increasingly diverse and complex sector. Together with business services, the financial services industry accounts for approaching 10% of the UK's economy. This is the largest contributed share to an economy of any country in the world. Financial firms offer a wide range of different services to business and private customers and have expanded and up-skilled their workforces over the past ten years.

Across the UK, around 40,000 people are working as customer services advisers in banks and building societies, which in total employ a workforce ten times that number. 128,000 people are registered as chartered accountants and many thousands more train as accounting technicians.

Today, all medium to large commercial and business organisations control their own finances, so there are many openings to work with financial data in schools and colleges, hospitals, shops and voluntary organisations, as well as in commerce and industry.

ACCOUNTANCY
Job opportunities

Accounting technicians work for accounting practices, industries and commercial businesses and in the public sector. They may work at entry level – similar to an accounts clerk – but, with qualifications and experience, can operate up to the level of a financial manager. A number are self-employed.

Accounting technicians keep financial records, check invoices, tax returns and wages. They make sure payments are made promptly and advise on bookkeeping, credit control and payroll systems. Working as part of an audit team they prepare and check figures for clients. Much of the work is similar to tasks performed by accountants, although there are jobs done by accountants that cannot be undertaken by accounting technicians.

Skills and qualities needed

Accounting technicians need confidence with numbers, good IT skills, an eye for detail and the ability to work with concentration under pressure. Also important are teamwork, good communication skills and determination.

Salaries

Rates of pay vary, but an accounting technician with a basic qualification can expect to earn around £14,000 per annum, while an experienced, fully qualified accounting technician is paid in the region of £25,000, depending on the company/organisation and location.

Prospects

With increasing numbers of organisations taking responsibility for their own finances, more jobs have been created for accounting technicians. Often, in small organisations they are the only trained financial staff. There are good opportunities for self-employment. Accounting technicians can study to become accountants, an accounting technician qualification giving exemption from part of accountancy training.

Ways into work

No formal academic qualifications are needed. Trainees must be over 16 years old and have a good standard of English and maths. Those with an A-level/Scottish Higher grade in Accounting or in two other subjects, or with a BTEC National Diploma in Business and Finance, are exempt from part of the training.

Apprenticeships and Advanced Apprenticeships are available (see Introduction). Accounting technician qualifications are linked to NVQs/SVQs in Accounting. Two organisations offer qualifications for accounting technicians: the Association of Accounting Technicians and the Association of Chartered Certified Accountants.

Finding a job

For information about Apprenticeships contact the Financial Sector Skills Council or your local Connexions/careers service which also holds information about local job openings for young entrants.

Job vacancies are advertised in local newspapers and in *Accounting Technician*, the monthly journal of the Association of Accounting Technicians.

CASE STUDY

Kevin Webber

'I did apply for university because that was what everyone else was doing, but I was half-hearted about it because I knew graduates with huge debts, struggling to find a decent job.

'For as long as I can remember I've enjoyed working with figures and I took A-levels in Maths, Computing and Technology.

'When I was at school I had a part-time job in a Safeway supermarket and after A-levels I worked there full-time while I decided what to do. There were good prospects with the supermarket. After two years I was an assistant controller, but when I saw a job in the local paper for an accounts trainee with the Colne Housing Society, offering the chance to work and study at the same time, I applied.

'I got the job and spent a day a week for the next three years studying at college, gaining NVQs at Levels 2, 3 and 4 and becoming a qualified Accounting Technician.

'At present I'm working for Puffa, the outdoor clothing company, as an assistant accountant. I'm studying in my own time for the Association of Chartered Certified Accountants exams and attend an evening class one night a week. It's hard work but the course is interesting and it certainly isn't all numbers. At the moment we're studying corporate business law, people management and information systems.

'In another three to four years I should be a qualified accountant. I'm ambitious and see a good career ahead, either working within a company or setting up my own practice.

'When I was at school my teachers expected me to go to university because that's what people did. I'm glad I made my own decision. I've never regretted not having a degree. I have no debts, an interesting job and excellent prospects. Many graduates would like to be in that position!'

BANKS AND BUILDING SOCIETIES

Today, most banks and building societies offer 24-hour, seven-days-a-week phone, internet or interactive television services. Both types of organisations now provide a wide range of financial services; both can arrange mortgages. The management and handling of customer services is increasingly important to banks and building societies as they try to persuade customers to buy more services from them.

Banking can be separated into:

- Clearing, retail and private banking – providing services for private customers
- Corporate and commercial banking – dealing with companies' finances
- Investment banking – covering investment management and advice.

Job opportunities

Banks and building societies have shed many work tasks which now can be performed online or via call centres. However, there will always be a need for some direct interaction with customers when advising on investment planning, obtaining business finance or exchanging currencies.

Bank/building society customer advisers sell financial services and deal with customer accounts, issue travellers' cheques and buy and sell currency. They are the first people customers meet. They usually begin employment as clerks or assistants, working behind the scenes on administrative tasks before dealing with customers.

Once accepted for a position with training, there are ample opportunities to learn the range of tasks undertaken, such as handling personal or business account deposits, payments and withdrawals, exchanging money, calculating interest charges on loan repayments and mortgages, setting up pension contributions and completing insurance plans.

Skills and qualities needed

Anyone working in a bank needs to be good with figures and have strong communication skills. It is essential to work well in a team and to be honest and reliable. A smart appearance and pleasant but businesslike manner are also important. Patience is essential. You'll need an eye for detail, plus a flair for selling.

Salaries

Rates of pay vary, but a bank or building society clerk can expect to start earning at around £11,000 a year – pay rising with responsibility and qualifications up to £30,000 for experienced customer service advisers with some management responsibilities. Companies offer staff mortgages and loans to employees at favourable rates.

Prospects

Promotion is based on performance. It can often mean a move to a different branch, which may mean relocation. A bank or building society customer service adviser can progress to trainee manager and bank manager. To move into management, a Diploma in Financial Services Management is needed.

Ways into work

There are no formal entry requirements, although many banks and building societies ask for four GCSEs/Scottish Standard grades A–C/1–3 including Maths and English Language. Apprenticeships are available (see Introduction), leading to NVQ/SVQ at Levels 2 or 3 in Providing Financial Services (Banks and Building Societies) and in Customer Service. Staff in banks and building societies may also be required to take formal Chartered Institute of Bankers (CIB)/Chartered Institute of Bankers in Scotland (CIOBS) modules or examinations.

Finding a job

For information about Apprenticeships contact your local Connexions/careers service, which also holds local job vacancies for young entrants.

Job vacancies are advertised in local newspapers/websites and useful careers information packs are available from all banks and building societies.

INSURANCE

There are two main areas of insurance: life and general.

Life insurance

People insure themselves so that if they become injured, critically ill or die, their family has financial support. Life policies can also be used to build up savings for retirement. Pension schemes come into this area of insurance, as do long-term investment contracts to fund retirement or children's education.

General insurance

Here, there are two areas in which individual entrants specialise: personal or commercial insurance; personal insurance deals with motor, travel, building and contents insurance – also, with accident cover; commercial insurance provides companies and employers with cover for all aspects of their operations.

Job opportunities

Insurance is a major industry, employing over 350,000 people in the UK. Job openings include:

- Insurance clerk – provides clerical assistance
- Insurance underwriter – issues policies
- Insurance broker – helps clients select and buy insurance policies
- Financial adviser – brings in new business, encourages people to plan for the future

- Insurance claims officer – checks claims to decide if they should be paid
- Insurance surveyor – assesses the degree of risk in a new insurance policy
- Insurance loss adjuster – investigates claims independently to decide if they are valid
- Risk manager – identifies risks, inspects premises and equipment to identify areas that might lead to loss or damage.

Only the first two job areas are open to new entrants.

Skills and qualities needed

Most insurance work involves contact with customers therefore staff should be smart in appearance with an efficient business manner and good communication skills. The ability to sell policies is important in many jobs, as is quick, clear thinking and a high level of organisation. All the work is performed on computers so excellent IT skills are necessary, as well an ability to work well in a team.

Salaries

Rates vary considerably, but average yearly salaries are:

- £12,000 for a clerk
- £20,000 for a claims official/an insurance broker/insurance surveyor
- £28,000 plus commission for a financial adviser
- £15,000 rising to £40,000 for an experienced insurance loss adjuster
- £21,000 to exceedingly high salaries for specialist risk managers.

Prospects

There are opportunities for staff to move into supervisory, team leader or management positions, as follows:

- Insurance clerks and insurance claims officials who are prepared to take Chartered Insurance Institute (CII) exams can become underwriters, brokers and financial advisers.
- Insurance brokers can move into risk management and loss adjustment.
- Underwriters may specialise in a particular area such as marine, aviation insurance or reinsurance, or move into surveying.
- Surveyors can move into underwriting or risk management.
- Financial advisers can move into senior posts or into areas such as marketing.
- Loss adjusters can specialise, or move into surveying or risk management.
- Risk managers often become self-employed or specialise in an area such as employee health, or fire risks.

Ways into work

There are no formal qualifications required to work in insurance, although many companies do expect good standards of education.

Apprenticeships are available (see Introduction) leading to NVQs/SVQs at Levels 2 or 3 in Insurance.

The following are typical qualifications that may be required by companies:

- Insurance clerk – four GCSEs/Scottish Standard grades including Maths and English. Clerks are encouraged to take the Certificate in Insurance awarded by the CII and also the Certificate in Insurance Practice.
- Insurance claims official – two to three A-levels, three to four Scottish Highers or the equivalent. Many companies promote insurance clerks to this level. Claims officials are usually expected to study for CII exams.
- Insurance broker – entry requirements are similar to those of a claims official. Brokers usually study for CII exams.
- Underwriter – entry requirements are similar to those for brokers. Underwriters are expected to pass the Advanced Diploma exams of the CII.

- Surveyor – A-levels or equivalent as above. Surveyors are expected to pass the Advanced Diploma exams of the CII.
- Financial adviser – employers tend to look for mature entrants for this area of work and expect financial advisers to achieve professional qualifications awarded by the CII or to pass the Institute of Financial Services exams.
- Loss adjuster – it is unusual for someone to go into loss adjustment straight from school. Qualifications are awarded by the Chartered Institute of Loss Adjusters (CILA).
- Risk manager – also a later career area, although some companies take on school leavers as junior technicians and move a few into risk management posts. Risk managers are expected to study for the Institute of Risk Management exams.

Major insurance employers

- AXA
- BUPA
- Legal and General
- Norwich Union
- Prudential
- Royal and Sun Alliance
- Standard Life
- TESCO Insurances
- Zurich Financial Services.

Finding a job

For information about Apprenticeship contact the Financial Sector Skills Council or your local Connexions/careers service which also holds local job opportunities for young work entrants.

Job vacancies are advertised in local newspapers/websites, on the Association of Accounting Technicians' (AAT) and insurance companies' websites and in professional publications such as *Financial Adviser*, *Money Management* and *Broker*.

USEFUL ADDRESSES

Accountancy work

AAT – Association of Accounting Technicians
140 Aldersgate Street
London EC1A 4HY
Tel: 020 7397 3000
www.aat.org.uk

ACCA UK – Association of Chartered Certified
Accountants
29 Lincoln's Inn Fields
London WCLA 3EE
Tel: 020 7059 5000
www.accaglobal.com

CIPFA – Chartered Institute of Public Finance and
Accountancy
3 Robert Street
London WC2N 6RL
Tel: 020 7543 5600
www.cipfa.org.uk
(CIPFA's Education and Training Information Service:
020 7543 5678)

Administrative/business

AMSPAR – Association of Medical Secretaries, Practice
Managers
Administrators and Receptionists
Tavistock House North
Tavistock Square
London WC1H 9LN
Tel: 020 7387 6005
www.amspar.co.uk

CfA – Council for Administration
6 Graphite Square
Vauxhall Walk
London SE11 5EE
Tel: 020 7091 9620
www.cfa.uk.com

City & Guilds
1 Giltspur Street
London EC1A 9DD
Tel: 020 7294 2800
www.city-and-guilds.com

Government Skills – Sector Skills Council for Central
Government
Cabinet Office
Admiralty Arch
Pall Mall
London SW1A 2WH
Tel: 020 7276 1611
www.government-skills.gov.uk

IAgSA – Institute of Agricultural Secretaries
and Administrators
National Agricultural Centre
Stoneleigh
Kenilworth CV8 2LG
Tel: 024 7669 6592
www.iagsa.co.uk

Institute of Legal Executives
Kempston Manor
Kempston MK42 7AB
Tel: 01234 841000
www.ilex.org.uk

Financial services – banks/building society work

Building Societies Association
6th Floor, York House
23 Kingsway
London WC2B 6UJ
Tel: 020 7437 0655
www.bsa.org.uk

FSSC – Financial Services Skills Council
51 Gresham Street
London EC2V 7HQ
Tel: 020 7216 7366
www.fssc.org.uk

IFS – Institute of Financial Services
IFS House
4–9 Burgate Lane
Canterbury CT1 2XJ
Tel: 01227 818609
www.ifslearning.com

Major UK banking firms have online careers pages:
www.jobsatabbey.com
www.barclays.co.uk/careers
www.bankofengland.co.uk/jobs
www.britannia.co.uk/careers
www.jobs.hsbc.co.uk
www.lloydstsbjobs.com
www.nationwide.co.uk/careers
www.rbs.co.uk/careers

Insurance work

CII – Chartered Insurance Institute
42–48 High Road
London E18 2JP
Tel: 020 8989 8464
www.cii.co.uk

CILA – Chartered Institute of Loss Adjusters
Warwick House
65–66 Queen Street
London EC4R 1EB
Tel: 020 7337 9960
www.cila.co.uk

PUBLICATIONS

Banking; *Securities and Investments*; *Accountancy: Chartered* are from the Inside Careers Guides series and can be down-loaded from www.insidecareers.co.uk

Chick in the City (CD-ROM for those with special needs) – 2006, Highflyers Publishing

How to Get Ahead in Business and Finance – 2006, Heine-mann, £12.99

How to Get Ahead in IT and Admin – 2006, Heinemann, £12.99

Working in Finance – 2006, DfES, downloadable from www.connexions-direct.com/wifinance

2 Art and Design, Multimedia, Advertising and Marketing

ART, DESIGN AND MULTIMEDIA

With continuous exposure to digitally enhanced images on web pages, TV and poster adverts, in films and videos, on book covers and packaging, in magazines and newspapers – today – we are all art and design critics! We are highly responsive to new images and new design in fashion, food presentation, multimedia accessories and interior furnishings.

The creative industries employ almost 2 million workers and contribute £12 million each year to the UK's economy – mainly through home sales and export of entertainment software, designer fashion, creative arts and TV programmes.

Growth is highest in leisure software and electronic publicity firms, but thousands of high-earning businesses are microfirms – self-employed enterprises where freelancers work for a few large companies with global reach. Design and multimedia companies have blossomed and there are growing opportunities for creative individuals with ability in the latest interactive digital technologies used for education and training products, entertainment resources and advertising.

Job opportunities

Of those in the creative and cultural skills sector, 33% work in London as creative artists, craft workers, designers, photo-imagists, website designers, interactive media, animators and special effects workers, broadcasters, publishers, electronic publicists or advertisers.

There are opportunities for designers in product design and packaging with publishing, advertising and multimedia companies right across the UK. London – with its large publishing houses, multiple advertising firms, fashion and textile houses, multimedia production enterprises, museums, galleries and antiques auctioneers, theatre, TV and film opportunities – offers the greatest range of openings.

Many young artists and designers are self-employed, producing iconic clothing, footwear and accessories, glassware and pottery which they sell from workshop hubs in design outlets. Some work as freelance graphic designers, producers of multimedia design applications and photo-imaging work.

CASE STUDY

Liam Phillips – Web Designer

It's not always straightforward to find means of support while spending all your time doing the thing you enjoy most or are passionate about, such as working in art and design.

Liam had always drawn since childhood, through his early teens, often developing elaborate, intricately designed scenes of fantasy battles between tiny armed figures. As he approached Level 3 studies, Liam decided to get a BTEC National Diploma qualification in Art and Design to qualify for a place on a well-recognised Foundation course in Art and Design which could catapult him into the Royal College of Art ... at the least!

'I started the BTEC course and chose the fine art strand, then added in multimedia. This was something completely new for me – a true artist. I had never dabbled in ICT developments. It was absorbing and time-consuming, but having found I could develop interactive games that other people found fun, using my own graphics, I was enchanted. This kind of artistic expression seemed to suit my skills and talents.

'When it was time for project work, I built a website with underpinning platforms carrying short interactive games I had designed and used it to advertise fruit tea.

'I took my design out around the business park, to friends' parents, to college staff, to the local Business Enterprise Fair. Everyone enjoyed playing on the site and I started to get website orders. I arranged to complete one work project for my coursework assignment and the venture just took off from there. I got to the end of the course, but I was already running my own web design business and – rather late in the day – learning how to manage the business side of the venture!

'I offer a fully managed service that covers webpage updates, maintenance and support, and many small businesses have signed up. The money I've made to date has been absorbed in developing my own software systems and some additional training in specialist programmes – but that's all essential investment!

I never did get to the Royal Academy, but that can wait for my old age.'

Skills and qualities needed

Jobs in this field all require imagination, creativity and vitality. This is a vocational sector where artistic entrants live and breathe their work, showing huge enthusiasm for new projects.

You need high levels of dexterity and have to be keenly observant with a sharp eye for detail. As much of the work is done under pressure to meet deadlines – often in unsocial hours – excellent focus and concentration is needed, plus the ability to work well on team projects. To be successful, you must have a strong interest in upcoming trends and fashions.

Jobs can require high levels of IT expertise with relevant software packages, perhaps in developing multimedia games or TV adverts, using computer-assisted design for new iPhones or packaging, or in setting the pages of a fashion magazine.

Roles in some firms require sharp business acumen – you might need to buy and sell, keep accounts, maintain portfolios and a client database, manage correspondence, do VAT and tax returns, run advertising campaigns and conduct market research.

Salaries

It's hard to give prospective salaries across the creative industries as there are large differences in the annual earnings of a desktop publisher for a small printing business, a freelance interior designer, a photo-imagist with an electronic publicist/advertiser, or a CAD-worker with a large motor vehicle company.

Starting salaries range from around £10,000 per annum for a sign-writer, through £14,000–£15,000 for DTP operator, to £16,000 for a product or website designer.

Experienced, highly qualified workers earn considerably more.

Prospects

All producers have to package, advertise and retail their goods and are continuously trying to improve on their usefulness or appeal. The majority of manufacturers use electronic publicists to advertise their products.

Globally, more and more companies sell via the internet, needing interactive and secure websites which are attractively designed and easy to navigate. Web designers can find openings with all larger manufacturers, printers and packing firms, clothing, textile and home furnishing companies. There is ongoing development and maintenance work for website builders, many of whom are freelance.

Fine artists, photographers and illustrators sell their own work, or are freelancers under contract to publishers, the Police Force, National Health Service, fashion and auction houses.

Multimedia firms may have small beginnings, but are often taken over or merged with larger businesses where there are economies of scale. Developing really exceptional training and educational films and videos, music videos, interactive computer games or promotional advertisements, contract work for multimedia designers can be highly rewarded. Large companies, advertising firms and government departments employ in-house multimedia teams to carry out their work.

Ways into work

If you enjoy art and design, multimedia or digital imaging and have five GCSEs/Scottish Standard grades A–C/1–3 including Art and Design, one route into work is to take a full-time one-year Foundation course at a college. Entry criteria vary and a few colleges require students to be 17 years old (some, even 18) or to already hold the equivalent of an A-level qualification. You need to have built up a suitable portfolio of your developing notebooks, sketches and completed artworks.

With GCSEs/Standard grades, colleges offer a range of courses leading to Level 3 qualifications: A-levels in Art and Design or Applied Art and Design; BTEC National Diplomas with a range of titles including Graphic Design, 3D Design, Textiles (with fashion), Fine Art, Film and TV Studies, Website Design and Multimedia.

From September 2008, 14–19 specialist Diploma courses start up in Creative and Media or ICT at Levels 1–3.

With an A-level/Scottish Higher qualification, a BTEC National qualification or a specialist Diploma at Level 3, you can take a college-based two-year Foundation degree in a particular creative area, tied with on-the-job learning with a local employer. Foundation degrees give guaranteed progression to an Honours degree but, alone, assist young designers to find appropriate paid work.

Although you don't need a degree to work in the creative industries, many employers consider courses leading to Level 3 qualifications provide essential underpinning art and design knowledge and skills. Multimedia and advertising firms appreciate qualifications accrediting skills in communication, ICT and use of English. Other organisations may seek qualifications in maths, accounting or business.

Finding a job

For information about Apprenticeships contact the Creative and Cultural Skills Council and, for the audiovisual industries, SkillSet or your local Connexions/careers service which has job opportunities for young work entrants.

Job vacancies are advertised in local newspapers/websites.

MARKETING

The job of a marketing department or agency is to identify customers' needs, research opportunities for products or services in the market, advise firms on product development and communicate information about products to customers, in order to increase sales.

For example, before a food company decides to develop a new range of organic fruity porridge oats, its marketing department carries out research into existing customer preferences, investigating possible gaps in the porridge market, and considers ways of promoting new products. Depending on the results of this research and a costs-projection exercise, the company might launch a new fruity porridge range supported by a marketing campaign including multimedia advertising, competitions and in-store promotions.

Job opportunities

Many large companies have their own marketing department, but others pay for the services of a specialist agency. With a post as a marketing assistant, if you took a Foundation degree in marketing, it could lead eventually to a position as a graduate marketing trainee.

Skills and qualities needed

Working in marketing needs strong communication skills, including listening very carefully to what a client is saying. Your portfolio of work can involve dealing with several different companies at the same time, so it is vital to be well organised. Imagination and enthusiasm are important, and so is the ability to work well as part of a team.

Salaries

A marketing trainee could expect to earn between £11,000 and £15,000 a year, while a market research manager for a motor vehicle company can be paid a salary approaching £40,000 annually. Senior marketing executives earn considerably more in firms with a global reach.

Ways into work

Most entrants are over 18 years old and usually hold a formal marketing qualification. The Chartered Institute of Marketing (CIM) awards qualifications at different levels:

- Introductory Certificate in Marketing – covers basic skills and is open to anyone over 17 years old with an interest in marketing who holds an NVQ/SVQ at Level 2 or four to five GCSEs/Scottish Standard grades at A–C/1–3.
- Professional Certificate in Marketing – can be taken by those over 18 years old who hold the Introductory Certificate and have a minimum of one year full-time experience in marketing.

There are higher-level qualifications for those with considerable experience in marketing and a degree or equivalent-level qualification.

Study for these qualifications can be full- or part-time, intensive, online or by distance learning. Further information is available from CIM (see Useful addresses on page 29).

The Communication, Advertising and Marketing Education Foundation (CAM) offers a Diploma through assignment and examinations in five marketing areas. Minimum entry requirements are five GCSEs/Scottish Standard grades A–C/1–3, including Maths and English language.

Individuals completing the Diploma can go on to take higher-level CAM qualifications. Again, study methods are flexible, including evening classes and distance learning. To find out more, contact CAM direct (see Useful addresses).

Finding a job

Further information about a career in marketing is available from local Connexions/careers offices. Vacancies for jobs with training are likely to be advertised in the local press and in specialist publications such as:

- *Campaign* at www.brandrepublic.com/campaign/
- *Marketing* at www.brandrepublic.com/marketing/
- *Marketing Week* at www.marketingweek.co.uk

CASE STUDY

Julian Thompson – Business Development Manager with Guardian Direct Marketing

Aged 27, Julian left school with A-levels in Sociology, Economics and History intending to go to university. Julian explains,

'I liked the idea of going to university, but couldn't decide what to study, so I took a year out, worked for a removal company and travelled in the States. On my return I did some selling – both door to door and telesales. The experience was great, but I wasn't earning enough to survive and needed a steady job.

'I applied for a job in the warehouse at Guardian, but didn't get it! A few days later I had a call. Someone had read my CV, noticed my sales experience and wondered if I'd be interested in a job as a sales executive. The pay was low, but the job had possibilities so I took it. In six years the job has grown and so have I. We work for some impressive clients – football clubs, television companies, national newspapers, multinational companies – our range of services is growing all the time.

'We organise print buying, mail out material and run a data capture service, analysing reader response to competitions or special offers. We now have our own creative department.

'I've been sent on a number of training courses and gained a BTEC Certificate in Business through evening classes.

'What I like about my job is that I feel valued and that my opinion is heard. If I'd got the warehouse job heaven knows where I'd be!'

ADVERTISING

Advertisements on TV, radio, posters, web pages and in the press inform people about the existence of a product or a service and try to influence their opinion on it. In the case of an ice cream or a holiday the aim of the advertisement is to persuade people to buy it, but that is not always the case. Charities advertise to stimulate people to donate to a cause; political parties advertise in order to attract votes. The government is the largest advertiser in the country and spends millions on recruitment and information campaigns about health and safety or work.

Job opportunities

Most advertisers put their advertising campaigns into the hands of a specialist agency, which does the entire job, from designing the advertisements to producing them and placing them with the media, for example, in newspapers and on TV.

There are:

Creative jobs
- Copywriter – writing the words for the advertisements.
- Art director – designing the advertisements.

Production jobs
- Traffic – in charge of ensuring that departments work together and the campaign keeps to schedule.
- Epro (electronic production) – working on sophisticated computer programs to produce the final material.

Account jobs
- Account planning – deciding the strategies needed for a successful campaign, carrying out research into existing customers and looking at ways to attract new ones. Account planners are involved throughout a campaign, making sure original aims are not lost and clients' needs are met.
- Media buying – deciding where and when an advertisement is to be placed and buying TV, newspaper or display space. Prices vary immensely and media executives have to negotiate the best deal possible.
- Account executive – bringing in work, meeting potential clients, giving presentations. Once a contract has been won, account executives keep in regular contact with clients, informing them on progress and reporting back to colleagues.

Skills and qualities needed

Energy, enthusiasm and the ability to work as part of a team are vital, as are tact and a sense of humour. Good communication skills also are essential, along with an organised attitude to work. You need to have an eye for design and an awareness of fashion trends.

Salaries

Pay levels vary greatly according to the size of the company and its geographical position. Trainee copywriters can start on salaries of around £17,000. Top salaries for successful advertising personnel often reach six figures.

Ways into work

There are no set entry requirements. Colleges offer a range of full- and part-time courses in advertising, business, media and communications which prepare students for a career in advertising but do not guarantee a job.

On-the-job training is available in the form of NVQs/SVQs at Levels 3 and 4 in Advertising and Public Relations.

The Communication, Advertising and Marketing Education Foundation (CAM) runs six Advanced Certificate courses (see section on Marketing) in which it is possible to specialise in advertising. The Institute of Practitioners in Advertising offers training courses for staff in some agencies.

Finding a job

The Advertising Association has a useful publication on its website called *Getting into Advertising* plus a recommended reading list. The Institute of Practitioners in Advertising website also has tips about finding a job.

Further information about a career in marketing is available from local Connexions/careers offices. Vacancies for jobs with training are likely to be advertised in the local press, but also in specialist publications such as *Adline, Campaign, Marketing* and *Marketing Week*.

USEFUL ADDRESSES

Advertising

Advertising Association
7th Floor North, Artillery House
11–19 Artillery Row
London SW1P 1RT
Tel: 020 7340 1100
www.adassoc.org.uk (look in Information Centre for *Getting into Advertising*)

Communication, Advertising and Marketing Education Foundation (CAM)
Moor Hall
Cookham
Maidenhead SL6 9QH
Tel: 01628 427120
www.camfoundation.com

IPA – The Institute of Practitioners in Advertising
44 Belgrave Square
London SW1X 8QS
Tel: 020 7235 7020
www.ipa.co.uk

Art, design and multimedia

Creative and Cultural Skills (Sector Skills Council)
4th Floor, Lafone House
The Leathermarket
Weston Street
London SE1 3HN
Tel: 020 7015 1800
www.ccskills.org.uk

Design Council
34 Bow Street
London WC2E 7DL
Tel: 020 7420 5200
www.designcouncil.org.uk

Marketing

Chartered Institute of Marketing (CIM)
Moor Hall
Cookham
Maidenhead SL6 9GH
Tel: 01628 427500
www.cim.co.uk

Communication, Advertising and Marketing Education
Foundation (CAM)
Moor Hall
Cookham
Maidenhead SL6 9GH
Tel: 01628 427120
www.camfoundation.com

Other useful websites:

There are several dedicated job search websites for creative
workers:
www.artshub.co.uk
www.artsjobsonline.com
www.artsculturemediajobs.com
www.workstation.co.uk
www.britisharts.co.uk/jobs.htm
www.printweek.com/jobs
www.digitalartsonline.co.uk
www.festivus.co.uk for jobs in animation

PUBLICATIONS

Art & Design Directory 2008 – Inspiring Futures Foundation, Westminster House, Kew Road, Richmond TW9 2ND, Tel: 020 8334 1600, www.trotman.co.uk

Media Uncovered – 2nd edition, 2007, Trotman, £11.99

The Creative Handbook – an up-to-date directory of photographers is obtainable from www.chb.com

The Design Council produces a useful (but dated) free booklet downloadable from www.yourcreativefuture.org

Working in Fashion and Clothing – 2006, DfES, downloadable from www.connexions-direct.com/winfashion

3 Computing and IT

Sixty years ago, the first electrical machine capable of computing or processing data was developed. Today, every UK organisation or firm relies on IT (information technology) to support its work. From sourcing essential materials, planning and carrying out tasks, running machinery and vehicles, to recording personal data, advertising and selling – computers are at the centre of operations.

Restaurants and pubs run computerised stock control systems and order supplies online; insurance companies, banks and government departments keep customer account details on secure computer databases; newspaper, magazine and book pages are designed on-screen and printed electronically; town planners use software programs to develop urban plans and to design traffic flow systems; music is composed and distributed through IT programs.

More than 1.25 million people work as IT professionals in the UK – 4% of the workforce in 2007 – with just under half employed in the IT industry itself. To keep up with present demand and new developments, about 200,000 additional professionals will be required each year for the foreseeable future!

IT

Job opportunities

Widespread use of computers has opened up numerous job opportunities, not only with IT companies, but across production, retail and travel operations, multimedia businesses, voluntary organisations, universities and hospitals.

IT is a fast-moving industry, which means job openings are constantly changing and developing. Across the broad IT field, jobs fall roughly into four groups:

- IT operations
- IT services

- IT sales and marketing
- IT research and development.

Many IT jobs require high-level skills and qualifications, but there are ways into the industry with Level 2/3 qualifications where you do further on-the-job training.

These roles include entering data, technical support or IT trouble-shooting, sales and customer service, training a company's workforce in the use of particular software packages, and supporting development of software and hardware systems.

IT operations

Large organisations run their own IT networks and systems, supported by an in-company IT operations department. Activities include helping staff members with computer problems, making sure the systems run efficiently, upgrading programs and researching future developments to meet the changing needs of the organisation.

Jobs in IT operations include:

- VDU (visual display unit) operator – entering data and word processing
- Database administrator
- Applications programmer
- Systems analyst and designer
- Network manager.

IT services

Currently people 68,000 work in IT technical support roles across UK organisations. However, many firms and organisations do not have their own specialist IT department. Instead, they contract with a specialist company to do essential work. Even businesses with a specialist IT department may buy-in the services of an IT company for specific tasks. Typical customers might be a hotel wanting a new website with secure online booking and payment facilities, a gas company upgrading its emergency call system or a firm requiring an extended customer database to offer global services.

IT service companies vary enormously and offer a wide range of activities: developing websites, designing and installing IT systems, managing particular projects and looking after customers' problems with both software and hardware.

Job opportunities include:

- Technical support staff/helpdesk operator
- Software support professional
- Project manager
- IT consultant
- Technical architect
- Hardware engineer.

IT sales and marketing

Individuals and organisations are constantly upgrading their IT systems and introducing new software packages. This provides opportunities for workers who combine technical know-how with selling and customer service skills. IT sales specialists visit potential customers to introduce their company's products and services. They listen to a customer's requirements and discuss how these could be met.

The work involves analysing an organisation's needs and coming up with a suitable IT solution, writing proposals explaining their recommendations and negotiating a sales contract with the customer.

Job opportunities include:

- Technical sales specialist
- Client manager
- Marketing professional.

IT research and development (R&D)

The pressure to develop new products is huge. Workers in R&D try to predict future needs and trends across the IT industry and then proactively develop solutions. The work includes developing new software and hardware products, testing new features, recognising and correcting faults before a product is on the market and writing user instruction manuals for new products. These jobs are for highly experienced IT workers, but they require less-qualified assistants!

Typical jobs are:

- Software developer
- Software engineer
- Product tester
- Technical author.

Skills and qualities needed

A fascination for information technology and ongoing developments is a basic requirement, but an IT specialist needs to be a logical thinker and an excellent analyst who enjoys problem-solving. Creative imagination is a plus for IT workers, who also need to be clear communicators who can explain technical matters in simple terms. Often, the work has to be done at speed and deadlines must be met, so it's necessary to work well within a team, often outside normal business hours.

Salaries

Salaries vary enormously from firm to firm and from area to area. A computer operator with word-processing and database skills is likely to earn in the region of £12,000 per annum. A technical support worker can earn from £13,500 to £20,000 annually, while a systems analyst/manager earns anything between £25,000 and £40,000+. Heads of IT divisions are paid in the region of £55,000+ annually.

Prospects

There are plenty of opportunities to progress in IT for those prepared to work hard and keep up-to-date with new developments. Higher-level qualifications and project experience are vital to career progression. If you have an excellent track record, promotion to senior and management posts can be very rapid.

Although there are openings for IT specialists in every part of the country, most advertised jobs are in London and the south-east. Working abroad is a possibility for someone with modern language skills, the right qualifications and experience. Huge numbers of employers across the UK and Europe will continue to need skilled IT employees.

Major IT employers

- Microsoft
- IBM
- Oracle
- Motorola
- Vodafone.

Banks and insurance companies, local government offices, retail organisations, food and drink distributors, manufacturers, hospitals and research organisations all advertise jobs – in fact, most sizeable operations in the UK have openings for IT specialists.

Ways into work

If you're seeking a job where you'll need to use software packages, employers welcome qualifications such as a British Computer Society's European Computer Driving Licence or CLAiT qualifications – certificates and Diploma at Levels 1–3 for IT users. Look through course prospectuses of your local colleges.

Apprenticeships (see Introduction) leading to NVQs/SVQs Levels 2–3 are available for young people in:

- Using IT
- IT services and development.

There are NVQs/SVQs at Levels 1–4 in IT-related subjects.

BTEC First and National Diploma and Certificate courses in Computer Science or Information Technology are run by most local colleges. Entry requirements are usually four GCSEs/Scottish Standard grades A–C/1–3.

A-levels in Applied ICT and Computing are offered at many schools and colleges.

Finding a job

For information about Apprenticeships contact your local Connexions/careers service which also holds local job opportunities for young work entrants.

IT jobs with training are often advertised in local newspapers, but there are excellent IT job websites (see below).

CASE STUDY

Tom Sewell

Tom is a service engineer in the IT department of a county council. He is 19 years old and joined the organisation as an Apprentice when he was 17.

'I work in a team of 17 people and, together, we look after all the computing systems of the entire council. Calls come through from the helpdesk and are entered into a logging system. A couple of people in the team are responsible for allocating jobs. Some cases involve travel to different offices across the county. I'm hoping to pass my driving test very soon, which means I will be able to go out on such calls.

'There are thousands of computer users looking to us for help. The most frequently logged problem is users forgetting their password. This can be put right from our desks, but first we have to carry out security checks to confirm the request is genuine and the callers are who they say they are.

'Computers have fascinated me since I was around 5 years old. I spent a year in the sixth form studying for an AS in Business Studies and then joined the council. Several months into my Apprenticeship I became fully employed which meant I started to earn good money. I shall finish my Apprenticeship in a few months and I am already qualified to work on Microsoft systems.

'The most satisfying part of my job is tackling a problem and finding the answer!'

USEFUL ADDRESSES

Information technology

British Computer Society
1st Floor, Block D
North Star House
North Star Avenue
Swindon SN2 1FA
Tel: 01793 417417
www.bcs.org.uk

e-skills UK – Sector Skills Council for IT
1 Castle Lane
London SW1E 6DR
Tel: 020 7963 8920
www.e-skills.com/careers

Help Desk Institute
21 High Street
Green Street
Orpington BR6 6BG
Tel: 01689 889100
www.hdi-europe.com

Institute of IT Training
Westwood House
Westwood Business Park
Coventry CV4 8HS
Tel: 0845 0068 858
www.iit.org.uk

Other useful websites

www.career-in-IT.co.uk
www.it-jobbank.co.uk
www.jobsite.co.uk

PUBLICATIONS

Inside Careers Guide series: *Information Technology*, downloadable if registered on: www.insidecareers.co.uk

Working in Computers and IT – 2006, DfES, downloadable from www.connexions-direct.com/wicomputersandit

4 Construction, Engineering and Production

In this wide field, there is a wealth of practical hands-on jobs with high quality training offering plenty of opportunities for promotion and career development! Over 8 million people are employed in these broad sectors of industry – over a quarter of the UK's active workforce!

As considerable numbers of the present workforce reach retirement age, there is a real need for enthusiastic young people of both sexes to enter these industries. Employers provide good-quality training and the opportunities for promotion that young people look for.

CONSTRUCTION

The construction industry employs around 8% of the UK workforce in building new homes, schools, offices, hospitals, roads, tunnels and railways and also in repair, renovation and refurbishment work. Extensive new-build projects to increase housing stock and develop schools are underway across Britain, besides major construction work for the 2012 London Olympics! There are ample opportunities for entrants to train in this industry.

Job opportunities

Full information about the wide range of craft and technician career opportunities is available from Construction Skills, the Sector Skills Council for the Construction industry.

Skilled craft careers include:

- Bricklayer
- Carpenter and joiner
- Floor layer
- Glazier
- Painter

- Plasterer
- Plumber
- Roofer
- Scaffolder
- Stonemason
- Tiler.

Technicians are the people behind the action on a building site. Their work is specialised and covers many different roles, including:

- Building technicians – whose work is often divided between site and office, supervising operations, drawing up plans and documents
- Civil engineering technicians – work on site and in the office, constructing roads, bridges, tunnels and all types of civil engineering projects
- Engineering construction technicians – follow plans to assemble engineering plants
- Estimators and quantity surveyors – cost out projects, putting together estimates for possible future work
- Buyers – negotiate the cost and delivery of materials needed for building projects
- Plant engineering technicians – buy, hire and organise construction plant and equipment used on site
- Site engineering and surveying technicians – measure and prepare the site for construction, interpreting specialist plans and drawings.

Skills and qualities needed

Craft personnel in the construction industry need to enjoy practical, creative activities and must have an eye for detail. Construction workers must have some ability with numbers and reading plans to follow and carry out instructions. Although it is necessary to work independently at times, construction workers usually work as part of a team and so have to get on well with people. Construction workers need stamina and good coordination; sometimes, working at heights. Safety is an important issue and a mature attitude towards work is essential.

Salaries

Apprentice salaries start at £160 a week. An operative worker, aged over 18, but without recognised training, earns around £12,750 per annum; a skilled construction craftsperson's salary is in the region of £15,000–£25,000 per annum, depending on experience. A construction technician's salary can range between £14,000 and £25,000 per annum; managers can earn £40,000+.

Prospects

Opportunities in the construction industry are very good. Craftspeople can progress to supervisory and management posts and so can technicians. There are excellent openings for self-employment. Qualifications can lead to construction-related Foundation (later, Honours) degrees.

Ways into work

Craft

The construction industry has a training scheme called the Construction Apprenticeship Scheme, open to all young people from the age of 16. It complements the government's Apprenticeship programme, lasts for around three years and leads to NVQs/SVQs at Levels 3 or 4 in a chosen craft.

Technician

It is possible to train at craft level and use the qualification to move on to technician training. To start on the Building Industry Technical Training scheme straight from school, a minimum of four GCSEs/Scottish Standard grades A–C/1–3, preferably including English, Maths and Science, is needed. It is also possible to begin training after a course equivalent to A-levels. Training leads to an NVQ/SVQ at Level 3 or 4. If you don't have the required qualifications but want direct entry to technician-level training, you can study at a college to obtain a qualification:

- 14–19 specialised Diploma in Construction (available from September 2008 at Levels 1, 2 and 3)
- An Applied A-level in Construction and the Built Environment
- BTEC/SCOTVEC National qualification in Construction.

Finding a job

For information about Apprenticeships contact your local Connexions/careers service which also holds local job opportunities for those aged 16–19.

ConstructionSkills, can help with work experience placements, site visits and careers materials. It also helps to find local employers for young people who wish to train. For more information on careers in construction, or to apply for an Apprenticeship, visit www.bconstructive.co.uk

CASE STUDY

Matthew Dunlop

Aged 21, Matthew is already an assistant site manager on a large housing development in Docklands in London.

After taking his GCSEs he was unsure what to do and 'dithered' for a while, before becoming an Apprentice with a specialist refurbishment company and taking an NVQ Level 1 in Bricklaying.

Matthew then transferred to Barratt, a national building company, where he went on to complete his Apprenticeship, gaining NVQ Levels 2 and 3. During that time he represented his college in a national bricklaying competition.

Matthew's managers at Barratt could see he had both talent and commitment and so they signed him for a two-year day release Ordinary National Certificate (ONC) course in Site Management. Matthew has nearly completed the Level 3 ONC course and is now working as an assistant to a senior site manager.

Matthew says,

'I'm quite an organised person and I like dealing with people. I really enjoy bricklaying but I am ambitious and keen to be a site manager.'

He is one of around 400 Apprentices working for Barratt across the country, and his bosses say that if Matthew continues as he started, he could work his way up to director level with the company.

ENGINEERING

Engineering is the process of researching, designing, developing and testing new technology underpinning today's transport, infrastructural and product developments. This is a global field of operation and UK qualifications are recognised by employers worldwide. With Europe, USA, Russia, India, China and other developing countries seeking technological answers to global warming, engineering opportunities are rising.

Job opportunities

Today, nearly 2 million people in the UK work in engineering (including automotive engineering) and there are plenty of excellent job opportunities. Engineering covers a wide range of different areas. Some of the main ones are:

- Manufacturing engineering – developing and using technology to change raw materials into manufactured products
- Control engineering – designing and making robots, switches, satellite tracking systems, the technology that runs the modern world
- Electronic engineering – using electrons to power the working of control equipment such as computers, telecommunications apparatus, microprocessors and technology using electronic circuits
- Electrical engineering – generating and supplying electricity from power stations, producing transformers, generators and cables

- Chemical engineering – finding technological solutions to changing raw materials into useful products such as plastics, paints, medicines and fabrics
- Mechanical engineering – working with all types of moving machinery
- Marine engineering – designing and building sea transport
- Aeronautical engineering – designing and building air transport, such as Airbus UK
- Nano-engineering – working on the design of sub-molecular sized tools
- civil and structural engineering – designing and building structures such as the 2012 Olympic stadium or the Channel Tunnel
- Automotive or motor vehicle engineering – designing and building motor vehicle prototypes, producing finished vehicles, diagnostic and repair work
- Agricultural engineering – developing, testing, producing, installing and maintaining large machinery for use on farms.

Skills and qualities needed

Engineers need a practical, enquiring mind and fascination in how things work. They need to enjoy science and work with numbers, and relish the challenge of finding solutions to problems. Engineers need to pay close attention to detail and to work accurately. They may work away from home, travelling long distances to work sites which can be in unsocial settings (exploration sites, oil rigs etc). They must be able to work on their own initiative but also need to enjoy working as part of a team. Engineers have to stay calm when problems arise.

Salaries

Pay levels vary a great deal from company to company. As a rough guide, an engineering technician earns around £14,000 per annum, rising with experience in the work. An incorporated engineer who has gained higher qualifications and considerable experience in the work can earn from £30,000 to £40,000 annually.

Prospects

With time in this work there are excellent opportunities to gain a recognised engineering qualification and to continue training to whatever level you wish.

The Engineering Council awards the following qualifications:

- Engineering Technician – to individuals completing an Advanced Apprenticeship, BTEC National Certificate or Diploma or approved NVQ/SVQ Level 3 and also to those who have a minimum of two years' approved training plus two years' experience in a responsible position.
- Incorporated Engineer – to degree graduates, people with HND/C plus further learning, a minimum of two years' approved training and two years' experience in a responsible position.
- Chartered Engineer – some Advanced Apprentices may go on to take a relevant degree that would enable them, with appropriate professional development, to obtain chartered status. Many engineers move into management roles or into non-technical jobs such as marketing, sales or finance.

Ways into work

Apprenticeships are an excellent way to begin an engineering career. An Apprenticeship lasts around two years and leads to an NVQ/SVQ Level 2. Entry requirements vary. Some employers ask for three/five average GCSEs/Scottish Standard grades, while others seek interest and commitment rather than academic qualifications.

An Advanced Apprenticeship leads to an NVQ/SVQ at Level 3 or 4, plus a Technical Certificate, and takes three to four years to complete. It involves both off- and on-the-job training with part-time academic study. Entry requirements are usually four GCSEs/Scottish Standard grades A–C/1–3 including Maths, English and Science or Design Technology. Although not essential, a GCSE in a modern foreign language can be helpful to an engineer. After completing an Advanced Apprenticeship it is possible to go on to university and take a degree in engineering, although NVQs/SVQs are available at Levels 4–5 in engineering.

For those wanting to study full-time, there is a wide choice of engineering courses on offer at colleges across the country. A good way to start is with a general course, such as electrical and electronic engineering, automotive engineering, mechanical or production engineering.

BTEC programmes (not in Scotland) can be studied full- or part-time, occasionally at the same time as an Apprenticeship. The work involves both practice and theory:

- BTEC First Certificate or Diploma – may require GCSE/Scottish Standard grade passes in Maths and Science
- BTEC National Certificate or Diploma – entry requirements are likely to be four GCSEs/Scottish Standard grades A–C/1–3
- BTEC Higher National Diploma or Certificate – requires National Certificate or Diploma or an equivalent qualification.

14–19 specialised Diplomas in Engineering will be taught in some further education colleges from September 2008. They will have a high practical content:

- Level 1 – studied at school with release to college for those aged 14 and 16
- Level 2 – studied at college, equivalent to five GCSEs/Scottish Standard grades A–C/1–3
- Level 3 – entry requirements are four GCSEs/Scottish Standard grades A–C/1–3.

Course requirements vary widely and many colleges take a flexible approach, running their own internal aptitude tests and interviews. Anyone interested in studying engineering should contact a number of local colleges to find out exactly what is on offer and the specific entry requirements for each course.

Finding a job

For information about Apprenticeships contact the local Connexions/careers service which also holds information about job opportunities for young work entrants.

It is a good idea to approach local firms directly about the possibility of a job with training. Vacancies are often advertised in local newspapers/websites.

SEMTA, the Sector Skills Council for Science, Engineering and Manufacturing Technology Alliances, runs an Engineering Careers Information Service and a helpful website (see Useful addresses).

CASE STUDY

Jim Bluer – Motor Vehicle Engineer at Honda, Swindon

'If you'd asked me what I wanted from my studies, career or my life, couple of years ago I simply couldn't have told you. Now I've landed a good job which pays remarkably well and where my work team has the greatest fun – they are some of the best mates you could spend time with! I'm happy in what I'm doing, which is how I measure success.

'I thought about A-levels and university while I was at school, but only because it seemed the done thing. Some of the teachers had stressed that we wouldn't get anywhere if we missed A grades at GCSE and that kind of stuck. When you're 15 or 16, and are not getting As across all your subjects, it doesn't do much for your confidence. What they *should* tell you is that even if your grades are truly poor, it is possible to find plenty of good paying jobs out there where grades are not vital.

'With five GCSEs at grades A–C, there were loads of opportunities at college which interested me just as much as A-levels, and as it turned out, it was the best decision I made because

I learnt a huge amount and made some really good friends. I took and passed an Applied A-level in Engineering and got an NVQ Level 2 in Machining and Fitting.

'I then started an Advanced Apprenticeship in Engineering at Lafarge Cement, Westbury which combined on-the-job work with day release to college, but it just didn't work out. The working conditions were not the best and I couldn't always get away to college because of shift changes.

'When I saw Honda were advertising, I jumped at the chance, and, although I don't come across brilliantly on paper, I was fully on-the-ball at the interview. I was made a permanent member of their workforce within six weeks and now have a whole new raft of skills. I may even get a Foundation degree in the not-too-distant future! Oh yes, just a small perk – I was able to get a Honda with discount.'

PRODUCTION

The list of goods produced by the manufacturing industry in the UK is enormous: from food and drink, paper and clothing, to helicopters, pharmaceuticals, plastics, paints and chemicals. While traditional industries, such as heavy shipbuilding, motor vehicle production and clothing and shoe manufacturing have declined, newer high-tech industries have flourished. The nature of the work has also changed as processes have become more automated. Today, there are very few unskilled or semi-skilled jobs and many more at technician and professional levels.

Job opportunities

Over 4 million people are employed across the production industries doing tasks that include goods inward, machine operation, assembly, packing, administration, marketing, selling and accounts.

In production work, people are employed as production line supervisor, production manager/controller, maintenance engineer, tool room worker, designer, quality control manager, laboratory technician, product researcher (also see section on Engineering in this chapter, and Chapter 13 on Science).

Skills and qualities needed

Production operatives need to work quickly and methodically, be reliable workers, good timekeepers and team players.

Salaries

A manufacturing operative earns approximately £13,000–14,000 annually and a quality control operator earns £20,500 or more.

Ways into work

From September 2009, schools and colleges will offer the new 14–19 specialised Diploma in Manufacturing (see Introduction).

One of the newer areas in manufacturing training is in Business Improvement Techniques (or B-IT) at NVQ/SVQ Level 2.

Production operative

There are no minimum entry requirements for this work, although some companies have their own aptitude tests and initial training. NVQs/SVQs at Levels 1, 2 and 3 are established in a large number of industries including food and drink, glass, plastics and rubber. Apprenticeships are available in manufacturing.

Quality controller

The work varies from short visual checks to complicated laboratory tests using specialised equipment. Quality controllers carry out the tests and analyse the results they obtain.

Entry requirements vary across different industries. There are no minimum entry requirements and some people enter quality control after working in production.

Some companies recruit school leavers into quality control and may look for four GCSEs/Scottish Standard grades

A–C/1–3 including English, Maths and Science. Apprenticeships are available.

Industries with complex quality control systems usually recruit people with higher qualifications such as A-levels/Scottish Higher grades, BTEC National or Higher National Awards or equivalent qualifications. Some positions require degrees.

Many quality control personnel study for the City & Guilds (7430) Certificate in Quality Assurance by day release, block release or evening courses. There are no entry requirements for this course.

The Institute of Quality Assurance runs Diploma and Advanced Diploma Quality Assurance courses, for which there are no set entry requirements.

Prospects

There are opportunities to train to craft or technician level and move into supervisory or management positions or into quality control, transport, warehousing and distribution.

Finding a job

For information about Apprenticeships contact your local Connexions/careers service which also holds job opportunities for young work entrants.

See the local press/websites for company vacancies, or contact firms directly for information about jobs with training.

USEFUL ADDRESSES

Construction

ConstructionSkills – Sector Skills Council for
Construction
Bircham Newton
Kings Lynn PE31 6RH
Tel: 01485 577577
www.citb-constructionskills.co.uk

SummitSkills – Sector Skills Council for Building Services
Engineering
Vega House
Opal Drive
Fox Milne
Milton Keynes MK15 0DF
Tel: 01908 303960
www.summitskills.org.uk

Engineering

SEMTA – Science, Engineering and Manufacturing
Technology Alliance
(The Engineering Careers Information Service)
SEMTA House
14 Upton Road
Watford WD18 0JT
Tel: 01923 238441
www.semta.org.uk

Also useful for engineering careers:
www.enginuity.org.uk

Manufacturing

CQI – The Chartered Quality Institute
12 Grosvenor Crescent
London SW1X 7EE
Tel: 020 7245 6722
www.thecqi.org

Improve Ltd – Food and Drink Sector Skills Council
Providence House
Ground Floor
2 Innovation Close
Heslington
York YO10 5ZF
Tel: 0845 644 0448
www.improveltd.co.uk

National Skills Academy for Manufacturing
2410 Regents Court
The Crescent
Birmingham Business Park
Birmingham B37 7YE
Tel: 0121 717 6610
www.manufacturing.nsacademy.co.uk

PUBLICATIONS

Real Life Guide: Construction – 2nd edition, 2007, Trotman, £9.99

Real Life Guide: Electrician – 2nd edition, 2008, Trotman, £9.99

Real Life Guide: Motor Industry – 2nd edition, 2007, Trotman, £9.99

Real Life Guide: Plumbing – 2nd edition, 2007, Trotman, £9.99

So You Want to Work in Engineering – 2005, Hodder Wayland, £13.99

Working in the Built Environment and Construction – 2006, VT Lifeskills, £8.50

Working in Electrical and Electronic Engineering; Working in Manufacturing – 2006, DfES, can be downloaded from www.connexions-direct.com/wi

5 Education and Training

To be ready to teach or train others, whether it's young children, adults or older learners, requires a certain level of maturity. This is not a job area that many 17 and 18 year olds consider. Most young people are just developing the balanced, confident outlook, consistency in self-organisation, reliability and high degree of responsibility for others that this work demands. There are always exceptions and you – the reader – might be of mature disposition, with a good general educational background, plus experience and knowledge of a specialist subject area, and yet have no degree.

If you have cared for someone yourself or have a keen interest in children, you may understand explicitly the demands of this work area and yet be interested and willing to gain the necessary experience and essential qualifications. You may be taking Level 3 qualifications and considering a teaching career, yet want to gain a taste of the work and find out if it's for you!

There are openings for those without degrees to get involved with training or teaching as assistants. Across the UK there are several hundred thousand people contributing to teaching and learning at this level.

CHILDCARE

For those working in childcare – from childminders, pre-school group assistants, play leaders to nursery nurses – there is increased emphasis on high-level training for the role and on health and safety awareness. Today, training includes working in a range of different situations, together with other professionals, parents and families, learning to provide the best care and early years' education for children.

Job opportunities

The need for parents to work has resulted in increasing demand for pre-school childcare, before and after school and holiday clubs. Government spending through its Sure Start programme has increased funding available to provide children from as young as two years with nursery provision during normal working hours.

Childcare workers are employed as nursery nurses and nursery assistants and supervisors, pre-school leaders, crèche leaders, special educational needs support staff, nannies and childminders. The work is in nurseries, schools, family centres, leisure centres, shopping malls, hospitals, cruise liners and hotels.

Skills and qualities needed

Affection for children and an interest in their psychological, physical and social development is essential. The work demands concentration and an awareness of risks, stamina, a sense of humour, a flexible approach and the imagination to stimulate and amuse children.

Salaries

Rates of pay vary widely. You can start as a nursery assistant on the minimum wage, but a qualified nursery nurse can earn £15,500 per annum. Nannies earn variable wages – some, as much as £17,000 per annum. Those with management responsibilities and further qualifications can earn over £20,000 per annum.

Prospects

There are opportunities for promotion to supervisor and manager and for self-employment, setting up nurseries, playgroups and school clubs. People with an NVQ/SVQ Level 4 qualification in Early Years Care and Education can train as teachers through the Registered Teacher Scheme.

Ways into work

Childcare qualifications include:

- CACHE (Council for Awards in Children's Care and Education) Diploma in Childcare and Education – This two-year full-time (three-year part-time) course is run by further education colleges across the country. Entry requirements are usually two GCSEs/Scottish Standard grades at A–C/1–3 including English language.
- BTEC First Diploma in Caring – a one-year full-time course that gives students without GCSEs access to BTEC National qualifications.
- BTEC National Diploma – a two-year full-time course that requires four GCSEs/Scottish Standard grades A–C/1–3. Students with this qualification can work in childcare or continue in training to become a teacher, nurse or social worker.

There are NVQs/SVQs in Caring for Children and Young People at Levels 2–4 and Apprenticeships (see Introduction) are available.

Finding a job

Information on Apprenticeships is available from the local Connexions/careers service which can also give advice on careers in childcare and local job opportunities.

Posts are advertised in local papers, *The Times Educational Supplement*, *Nursery World* and *The Lady*.

CASE STUDY

Ryan Wakley

Aged 20, Ryan is in the final year of a two-year course leading to a National Nursery Examinations Board (NNEB) childcare qualification.

In Year 10, when everyone was choosing work experience options, Ryan chose to go into a school, partly because he liked young children, also because he wanted to find out what made teachers tick!

Work experience proved so enjoyable that Ryan decided to enter a career in childcare, taking an A-level in Health and Social Care at his local college.

Ryan's aim is to work with children aged between 3 and 5 and he has already spent some time working in a pre-school nursery class. Once qualified, Ryan sees himself working locally to gain experience before seeking a job further afield.

In his words,

> 'There are plenty of opportunities for travel with this qualification, so I'll see how I feel once I've found my feet. Meanwhile it's great working with young children and seeing them develop.'

TRAINING OR TEACHING

There are always openings for young and older adults without degrees to get involved with training or teaching as assistants. You might be taking Level 3 qualifications and considering a teaching career, yet want to spend a little time in a workplace setting to find out if it's for you! Though tough on occasions, if you enjoy interacting with children and young people, and have a real interest in helping to develop their social and wider skills and intellectual abilities, the work can be rewarding and fun. Across the UK, there are several hundred thousand people contributing to teaching and learning at this level.

Job opportunities

Younger people interested in education as a job area usually express interest in helping to train and teach pre-school age children, working as nursery or play-group assistants.

There are openings in primary schools for teaching assistants and you might find work as an assistant in a school for pupils with special needs.

With an interest in school-age children, you can gain hands-on experience through working in an after-school and holiday play scheme, or, by taking a job as a play worker in a recreation centre, holiday camp (UK or overseas), shopping mall, leisure centre, a hospital paediatric ward or health centre crèche.

Adolescents can be more challenging for young people to work with, but there is a need for teaching assistants in training centres, farms and horticultural centres for the disabled. Only older entrants would be considered for more demanding positions in youth offending centres, or for assisting delivery of creative therapy training in art, drama or music.

If you have a special talent or skill, you might wish to be an assistant – then train as a leader – in, as examples: outdoor activities, sign language or community arts, drama or dance, or work as a teacher of guitar, drums or keyboard, or as a sports coach.

Some skilled but unqualified teachers work part-time in adult community centres and colleges. There are many opportunities to help adults develop basic skills in reading, writing and number work.

Skills and qualities needed

All entrants to work with young children and adolescents need to have a Criminal Records Bureau disclosure check.

You cannot underestimate the degree of patience you will need, combined with an interest in young and older people's development, backed with clear communication, literacy and numeracy skills. Keen observation and an acute consciousness of safety are essential in this field. Having a good sense of humour and a lively, creative imagination will always help you to engage others in learning!

This is responsible work – the care of others and their development rests with you – so this demands reliability and dependability, plus a sense of purpose.

Salaries

The work is poorly paid, until, with higher qualifications, you achieve higher-level teaching assistant status (HLTA) or become a fully fledged nursery nurse, play worker, sports coach, etc.

As a teaching assistant, working full-time you could expect to start earning around £11,000 per annum, although this will rise with experience and further qualifications gained in the work, when you can expect to earn over £20,000 annually.

Temporary play workers in holiday camps or crèches in shopping centres will only earn the minimum wage for their age group.

Prospects

Plenty of teaching assistants and those who love nursery assistant work go on to become fully qualified, achieving Level 3 or higher qualifications. Experience in the work is valued and you could expect to reach a supervisory or management-level position in a nursery within a few years.

At present, there are far more openings with the Early Years programmes run by the Teaching Development Agency than for teaching adult learners.

HLTAs in primary schools can continue to gain qualifications leading to a professional role as a teacher with QTS (qualified teacher status). This requires a minimum of GCSE/ Scottish Standard grades at A–C/1–3 in English language, Maths and Science, before you move through Level 3, eventually to gain degree-level qualifications.

Teachers of Early Years programmes and qualified nursery nurses are sought by British schools, nurseries and families overseas.

Ways into the work

For education and training work, you will need GCSEs/ Scottish Standards in English language and Maths, sometimes at grades A–C/1–3. Work entrants might hold a Level 2 qualification in Health and Social Care. From September 2008, a specialised Diploma in Health and Social Care is available at Foundation level, Level 1.

For nursery or play work with children, it is useful to hold a BTEC First Diploma or National qualification in Children's Care Learning and Development, or a Level 1 or 2 of the tiered

CACHE qualifications in Child Care and Education or in Play Work. Once in a job, you can gain NVQ/SVQs at Levels 1 and 2 in Child Care.

An A-level/Scottish Higher in Health and Social Care would be a plus.

Some Apprenticeship opportunities may exist where you earn as you learn and gain NVQ qualifications to Level 3 (see Introduction).

For community centre teaching or training of adult learners, there is help with professional development and qualifications through Lifelong Learning UK (see Useful addresses).

Finding a job

For information about Apprenticeships, contact the local Connexions/careers service which has information about local job opportunities for 16–19 year olds.

Job vacancies with training are also advertised in local newspapers/websites.

Avoid positions with no clear opportunities for formal training to gain qualifications in the work.

Opportunities to teach basic skills to adults are advertised also on local college websites.

Magazines such as *The Lady or Nursery World* advertise nursery nurse positions – often abroad, and the *Times Educational Supplement* carries teaching assistant advertisements.

USEFUL ADDRESSES

Nursery nursing/childcare

CACHE – Council for Awards in Children's Care and Education
Beaufort House – Head Office
Grosvenor Road
St Albans AL1 3AW
Tel: 0845 3472123
www.cache.org.uk

Lifelong Learning UK – Sector Skills Council for Lifelong
Learning
5th Floor, St Andrew's House
St Andrew Street
London EC4A 3AY
Tel: 0870 757 7890
www.lifelonglearninguk.com

NCMA –National Childminding Association
Royal Court
81 Tweedy Road
Bromley BR1 1TG
Tel: 0845 880 0044
www.ncma.org.uk

Professional Association of Nursery Nurses
2 St James Court
Friar Gate
Derby DE1 1BT
Tel: 01332 372337
www.pat.org.uk

Scottish Childminding Association
Suite 3
7 Melville Terrace
Stirling FK8 2ND
Tel: 01786 445377
www.childminding.org

SkillsActive – The Sector Skills Council for Active Leisure
and Learning
Castlewood House
77–91 New Oxford Street
London WC1A 1PX
Tel: 020 7632 2000
www.skillsactive.com

TDA – The Training and Development Agency for Schools
151 Buckingham Palace Road
London SW1W 9SZ.
Teaching Information Line: 0845 6000 991
www.tda.gov.uk (has useful training information on the Support Staff pages)

Other useful websites

www.childcarecareers.gov.uk
www.lgtalent.com

PUBLICATIONS

Working in Schools and Colleges – 2006, VT Lifeskills, £8.50

6 Environment: Working with Animals and Plants

Through their work with living organisms and the natural environment – on which we all depend – around 1.1 million workers in the UK have direct contact with animals and plants. Their involvement may be in growing plant crops, providing biofuels, timber, fish, meat or dairy products, in caring for animals or in conserving natural landscapes and ecosystems.

Some workers help manage land use to protect wildlife and maintain natural habitats, while balancing the interests of farmers and those using the land for sport and recreation.

With advances in technology, numbers of jobs shrank and the emphasis of work in this sector changed, but there are new, significant opportunities for people interested in working either directly or indirectly with animals, plants and the natural environment.

ENVIRONMENT

Many young and older workers now seek 'green careers' – jobs which support sustainability in land management and where efforts are made to slow or reverse environmental changes contributing to loss of biodiversity on a global scale.

Today, the importance of reducing habitat degradation and halting climate change is widely recognised and reflected in an increasing need for environmental and conservation workers.

Reforms to the Common Agricultural Policy require producers and growers to protect wildlife and meet targets to sustain biodiversity. Also, farmers must tackle issues of sustainability in managing their land – so, many enterprises now have an environment conservation worker to help them meet government and EU directives.

These roles involve physically demanding, active outdoor work. Some have an element of office- or lab-based practice. All positions are richly rewarding in terms of job satisfaction but, below management level, are generally low-paid.

People who care about the natural world can enter this area of work with few or no formal qualifications – usually starting with volunteering posts where they gain skills, practical knowledge and experience while developing a network of contacts.

Job opportunities

'Green' job areas open to those with few formal qualifications arise with Wildlife Trusts, the National Trust, RSPB, Natural England, and sometimes with the Environment Agency, CEFAS and DEFRA. The Countryside Agency and many other organisations and individuals who manage parkland, forests, moors, fisheries and estates employ the following:

- Environmental conservation project worker – monitoring and assessment, habitat regeneration, reintroduction of native species
- Countryside warden/ranger – sampling and surveying, planting, fencing, informing the public
- Fisheries project management worker – sampling, monitoring, aquaculture trialling, reporting
- Agricultural environmental management worker – helping farmers meet biodiversity targets and tackle sustainable land use
- Game and wildlife warden – maintaining upland, woodland and wetland habitats for breeding game (partridge, pheasant, grouse and deer) for shooting-based field sports
- Trees and timber environmental project worker – forestry work to increase biodiversity and sustainability in timber production
- Land conservation project worker – helping to manage and sustain terrestrial, freshwater and maritime landscapes, monitoring plants and animals in sites of special scientific interest
- Landscape gardener – working to maximise the sustainability of plantings in national parkland
- Fencer – working with a variety of materials to create attractive barriers.

Skills and qualities needed

This work demands, besides an interest in nature, practical skills and good problem-solving ability. You should be able to work on own initiative, but also work well with others in a team. You'll need to be dextrous, have good eye-hand co-ordination and be physically fit, with stamina to be able to work outdoors in all weathers. Reliable workers are conscious of health and safety issues.

It helps if you have a clean driving licence; also, ICT skills for recording survey results.

CASE STUDY

Karen Robb – London Wildlife Trust Site Manager

'If you want to know why I am doing this job, it's because I haven't been able to think of another way I'd rather spend my time.

'At school, whenever it was possible, I dawdled about the edges of the playing field – in the hedges and by the River Crane. I did have friends, but they had to like what I was doing or they didn't get to see me.

'My real interest was living things – particularly small furry mammals, and it was not enough that our home was overflowing with dogs, cats, hamsters, rabbits and guinea pigs. I spent hours huddled over mice nests or trying to feed young rabbits on new diets when at home; at school, I tried to build rafts for water voles to climb out of over-brimming ditches and started burrows for them in the muddy banks. Sometimes rats used them instead, so I built defences to protect the voles.

'When other girls were revising their Spanish & Humanities, I was looking up problems with mink on the internet. At the end of Year 11, nothing could have persuaded me to stay on at school, if I hadn't realised I could take Biology as a separate A-level subject. Time in the classroom was dead time, as far as I was concerned.'

Karen completed and passed three A-levels but never considered taking a degree course. Besides her pets, Karen had developed an interest in birds and joined London's Wildfowl and Wetlands Trust volunteer force. There, Karen contributed all her spare time to the conservation of reed beds and wildfowl at Barnes Wetlands. With keen observational skills and interest in keeping records, Karen became a highly informative guide to school groups and indispensable to the Trust which, after three years, offered her a paid position. Financially, Karen was not much better off than as a stable-hand, but the post allowed her to share her enthusiasm with newcomers to the Wetlands and to do further ecological management, producing regular reports.

'My experience and learning was boosted by the expert wardens at London's Wildfowl & Wetlands Trust and I taught myself the underpinning science. It was very difficult to think of leaving the Wetlands, but I wanted to boost conservation of water voles higher up the Thames and so tried for the Wildlife Trust manager's post at Crane Park. I never thought they'd appoint someone without a degree, but they thought my projects and research reports had taken me to that level already! I've made films on conserving the ecology of the Thames and now aim to put all that into practice at Crane Park Island.

'I am tired by the end of a busy day, particularly if the weather has been a bit dour, but no one could be happier degree or no degree!'

Salaries

Starting out, you will only earn around £9,000 per annum, but with some experience in the work, and NVQs at Level 2 or 3, pay rises to £13,000.

Experienced rangers and project workers can earn £20,000. Managers and head wardens earn over £25,000 annually.

Prospects

Although no formal qualifications are needed for entry, environmental conservation work requires commitment and a dedicated approach to tasks. Almost all entrants start by gaining experience and knowledge through volunteering; salaried positions are usually only available to those who have completed six months' voluntary work. Those who enjoy and are successful in this work rise to become wardens and managers employed on large farms and estates and in countryside parks, some even being self-employed as environmental consultants.

Ways into work

At present, around 20,000 people of all ages are volunteer environmental conservation workers in the UK. Work experience helps you decide if this is the right career choice and whether the reality of the job matches your expectations!

Once in a volunteering post, you will receive health and safety training (possibly, also training in First Aid) and may be able to work towards NVQs/SVQs Level 1 and 2 in Environment Conservation. Some organisations offer Apprenticeships in Environment Conservation, where you are paid a salary to learn the skills, attaining NVQ/SVQ Level 2 and 3.

Starting with at least four GCSEs/SCEs at A–C/1–3, you could follow a part-time BTEC National Certificate in Countryside Management or Land and the Environment, while volunteering to gain practical experience.

In this field, there are always part-time opportunities for continuing your professional development and you can achieve degree level qualifications which include business-management skills.

Finding a job

There are 5,000 organisations with around 56,000 workers which advertise posts across the UK, so search the job vacancy pages of the main organisations offering volunteering opportunities listed below.

ANIMALS

The British are a nation of animal lovers! Many of us keep and look after animals as pets throughout our childhood or, are in daily contact with domesticated farm animals, while a few of us are highly knowledgeable about native wild animals: birds, mammals, fish, reptiles, amphibia and insects.

The changed nature of livestock farming and the reduced numbers of small- or medium-sized operations and improved technology has meant higher volumes of animals but fewer opportunities for livestock workers. However, there are many openings for young people to work with non-domesticated animals in zoos, captive-breeding/conservation or wildlife parks, on farms, in stables, farriers or fisheries, or in clinics, breeding centres, pet shops, animal homes and laboratories.

One third of the 75,000 UK livestock businesses have signed up to the government's environment protection scheme which means that farmers must spend at least 11 hours per week and some money on sustaining the natural environment – clearing ponds of vegetative growth, removing rubbish and noxious wastes, composting manure safely, improving fencing, planting woodland copses, replacing hedgerows etc. Some farmers employ environmental conservation workers (see above) on a part-time basis to assist them in planning and carrying out such tasks.

Animal welfare businesses employ 47,500 individuals across the UK today, but only 7,419 of this number are qualified as registered veterinary nurses with a further 3,781 in training at present. Around 50,000 people work with horses in a range of capacities and both areas of work can be entered with no formal qualifications.

Job opportunities

- Livestock agricultural worker – feeding, watering, herding, assessing, milking, dipping, assisting at calving or lambing time, shearing, docking, egg collecting/grading
- Livestock handler – moving and transporting bulls, rams, billy goats and other animals for slaughter, herding animals for milking
- Agricultural engineer – maintaining and repairing agricultural machinery, from milking machines to combine harvesters
- Stablehand – mucking out, feeding, watering, grooming, walking and exercising horses and ponies, taking horses to farrier for shoeing
- Animal care worker – handling and inoculating animals, caring for sick or post-operative animals, teaching animal care to pet owners

- Fisheries worker – feeding and inspecting fish in hatcheries, netting, moving and transporting fish to restock lakes and rivers or killing and boxing marketable fish
- Aquaculture worker – setting ropes and cages in marine lochs and estuaries to cultivate mussels, oysters and shellfish; harvesting, weighing and grading cultured organisms for market
- Dog groomer – clipping hair and nails of dogs
- Dog handler/walker/pet sitter – training dogs to respond to commands, exercising animals for kennels or owner
- Horse trainer's assistant – taking horses out on regular exercise rides
- Horse breeder's assistant – looking after animal studs used for artificial insemination purposes
- Animal technician – looking after animals bred under Home Office licence for testing, ensuring their care and well-being, performing routine treatments
- Poultry worker – feeding, watering, cleaning out, assessing, counting and moving hens, chicks, ducks, geese and turkeys.

Skills and qualities needed

This work essentially demands reliability and dependability. You need to be keenly observant and always complying with the health and safety regulations. Animal handlers are practical people with good problem solving skills. You may need to listen to and carry out instructions very carefully and it does help if you have experience in caring for animals! A calm, determined and practical approach to tasks, with a concerned but unsentimental attitude towards animals are musts.

You'll need stamina and not have to mind early starts and late finishes – working in all weathers and sometimes, unsociable hours!

Good teamwork skills are a plus and you'll need the ability to assess the animals and keep records. A clean driving licence will be useful.

Salaries and prospects

A downside of this work is that despite hours in work being long, the pay is low. Unless you own and breed successful race horses, have a herd of organically fed Aberdeen Angus cattle or are owner/manager of a breeding station, you will not become rich.

Pay starts at the minimum wage for those handling, caring for and feeding animals, but with experience and qualifications you can become a supervisor, even manager, of a herd or flock and earn over £21,000 per annum and up to £30,000 on some estates.

Ways into work

Considerable numbers of young people start as animal workers with few or no formal qualifications. Many individuals have early experience of animal-handling through having hamsters, dogs, cats, ponies or horses as pets and may be volunteers at a local cattery, dogs' home or kennels.

Having a regular volunteering slot means that you can build reliability and consistency of care, an important stepping-stone to getting a paid position or an Apprenticeship. There are NVQs/SVQs Levels 1 and 2 in Animal Care or Equine Studies, or to Level 3 in Horse Care and Horse Care Management and many colleges offer part- and full-time BTEC/SQA National qualifications at Level 3 in Animal or Horse Care, Equine Studies.

Agricultural colleges offer a full range of specialised courses and you might choose to take your learning to Level 4 and a Higher National Certificate or Diploma in your area of interest. Most work entrants study part-time and you should check that a potential employer will allow you time off for study and training.

Finding a job

For information about Apprenticeships contact your local Connexions/careers service which also holds local job opportunities.

Local Wildlife Trusts, RSPB societies, nature reserves, Wildfowl and Wetlands Centres and British Trust for Conservation Volunteers (BTCV) projects require volunteer workforces and this is where many start in environmental work. The tasks include conserving habitats and helping to build nesting sites for animals, insects, amphibian, reptiles, birds and mammals (species such as bats, water voles, red squirrel etc). Mucking out at your local stables or zoo is the way into paid work for others.

All societies advertise vacancies; try websites below to get a flavour of jobs on offer. Pet handlers, walkers, grooms and trainers are sought in local newspapers. Veterinary practices and farms advertise for assistants, farm and stablehands in job centres, the Connexions/careers service or in the local press/websites.

USEFUL ADDRESSES

British Horse Society
Stoneleigh Deer Park
Kenilworth CV8 2XZ
Tel: 08701 202244
www.bhs.org.uk

BTCV – British Trust for Conservation Volunteers
Sedum House
Mallard Way
Doncaster DN4 8DB
Tel: 01302 388 883
www.btcv.org.uk

CMA – Countryside Management Association
Writtle College
Lordship Road
Writtle
Chelmsford CM1 3RR
Tel: 01245 424116
www.countrysidemanagement.org.uk

Countryside Jobs Service – advertises paid and voluntary positions:
www.countryside-jobs.com

DEFRA – Department for Environment, Food &Rural Affairs
Customer Contact Centre
Eastbury House
30–34 Albert Embankment
London SE1 7TL
Tel: 020 7238 6951
www.defra.gov.uk

Environment Agency
National Customer Contact Centre
PO Box 544
Rotherham S60 1BY
Tel: 08708 506 506
www.environment-agency.gov.uk

Institute of Fisheries Management
22 Rushworth Avenue
West Bridgford
Nottingham NG2 7LF
Tel: 0115 982 2317
www.ifm.org.uk

Lantra – Sector Skills Council for the Land-Based Industries
Lantra House
Stoneleigh Park
Coventry CV8 2LG
Tel: 0845 707 8007
www.lantra.org.uk
also www.afuturein.com and www.ajobin.com

National Trust
PO Box 39
Warrington WA5 7WD
Tel: 0844 800 1895
www.nationaltrust.org.uk

Wildfowl & Wetlands Trust
Slimbridge
Gloucestershire GL2 7BT
Tel: 01453 891900
www.www.org.uk

Natural England
1 East Parade
Sheffield S1 2ET
Tel: 0114 241 8920
www.naturalengland.org.uk

RSPB – Royal Society for the Protection of Birds
The Lodge
Potton Road
Sandy SG19 2DL
Tel: 01767 680551
www.rspb.org.uk

The Wildlife Trusts
The Kiln
Waterside
Mather Road
Newark NG24 1WT
Tel: 01636 677711
www.wildlifetrusts.org

Other useful websites

www.endsjobsearch.co.uk/jobs/
www.animal-job.co.uk
www.growing-careers.com

PUBLICATIONS

Real Life Guide: Working with Animals and Wildlife – 2nd
    edition, 2008, Trotman, £9.99
Working in The Environment – 2006, VT Lifeskills, £8.50

7 Hair and Beauty

For increasing numbers of women and men, being well-groomed is a personal investment that can pay dividends. First impressions count! People realise that their external appearance radiates important messages. Care with dress, hair, make-up and nails sends out signals about your attention to detail, skills with time-management, your self-respect and the level of regard in which you hold clients and fellow-workers.

As we turn to beauty therapists, hairstylists and nail technicians, while more visit spas for facials and treatments, the numbers of UK workers in hair and beauty have soared above 300,000 and, are rising. Profits from the growing UK hair and beauty industry now reach over £3 billion a year.

Today, the only problem for salons managers and cosmetic retailers is in filling their vacancies for trained stylists and therapists. Their answer has been to treat present staff and unqualified entrants as vital assets – improving the quality and rigour of work-based training they offer. UK qualifications and awards are valued as the best in the world!

With rising status and pay for those gaining qualifications and experience, now is an excellent time to enter this industry, if you are ambitious and want to go to the top!

HAIR

Job opportunities

Hair stylist

Hairstyling is creative work which can be carried out on a flexible basis – in small or large salons, on film sets, in TV studios or theatres, in hotels, hospitals and care homes, on cruise liners, at clients' or your own home.

Over 230,000 people work in the hairdressing sector as their main or second job. There is:

- Hairstyling or barber work – advising on style, washing, conditioning, trimming, cutting, layering, colouring, perming, blow-drying, accessorising
- Hair removal – shaving, clipping, electrolysis, waxing, sugaring
- Hair regeneration – weaving, transplanting, wig making and fitting
- Trichology – diagnosing and treating hair and scalp problems.

Skills and qualities needed

Hairdressers need to be confident and outgoing, interested in others, get on well with all types of people. Clients need to be put at their ease, able to relax.

You need to be good with your hands, artistic and aware and interested in the latest fashion trends. Stylists need an eye for design and creative flair.

You should look smart and have the stamina to be on your feet all day.

Salaries

Apprentice stylists earn an annual salary of around £7,000. Advanced Apprentices earn £10,600. Experienced and qualified stylists can earn far more – usually, around £18,500 per year, rising to £30,000 in London salons, but top stylists earn over £40,000.

Hair and beauty workers receive tips which can boost their wages.

Prospects

Stylists at Level 3 may train further – taking professional qualifications to Level 4 – equivalent to an HND or Foundation degree – to become senior stylists and salon managers. Many stylists run their own businesses from home, many offering a mobile salon service.

Very competent managers can run UK-wide chains of salons, having gained additional professional qualifications at NVQ Level 5 or equivalent.

To stay ahead in this profession requires continuous upgrading of your skills and knowledge of new styles and products. Stylists attend fashion shows, exhibitions, company product promotions and training courses and often practise new skills in the salon, after hours. Some stylists take specialist qualifications such as African-Caribbean hairdressing or men's barbering. Some stylists also train in make-up techniques and go into the fashion or film industry.

Ways into work

Young people can enter hairdressing work with no formal qualifications, undertaking tasks such as sweeping up, making drinks and shampooing clients' hair. Having a Saturday or a part-time evening job can be a good way to find out if you like the work. Study local further education college prospectuses to see what courses are on offer.

With a few average GCSEs/Scottish Standard grades, Apprenticeships are available for entrants to hairdressing. Formal training, in the salon or through part-time study at College, leads to NVQs/SVQs at Levels 1 and 2: the minimum qualification standard for a junior stylist.

With Level 2 qualifications (four –five GCSEs/Scottish Standard grades at A–C/1–3, a BTEC First or NVQ Level 2), junior stylists – often as Advanced Apprentices – can work towards an NVQ Level 3 and stylist status.

Finding a job

For information about Apprenticeships contact the local Connexions/careers service which also holds local job opportunities for young work entrants.

Some colleges run their own job centres where local employers register vacancies.

Job vacancies are also advertised in local salons, newspapers/websites. Trade magazines carry job advertisements for top stylists.

BEAUTY

This is an industry which is raking in the profits! Younger and older males now seek pampering skin treatments – often, spa treatments/therapies. New products for males are filling bathroom shelves. Spas and salons are growing at a rate of 3% per annum.

Of course, females of every age also contribute to this trend which is leading to skills shortages across the beauty industry. As products and processes become more complex, demonstrators and beauty consultants require specialist training to pass on product knowledge.

With increased leisure, many people take short breaks and seek accommodation where spa and beauty treatments are available on site but, often, there is a lack of qualified staff to satisfy demand.

A considerable number of employers of beauty therapists operate microbusinesses that cannot afford to train new staff.

Job opportunities

Beauty therapist

Beauty therapists carry out treatments such as hair removal, lash and brow treatments, facial and body massage, and electrical treatments. Working in salons, cruise liners, store beauty departments and in clients' homes, there are opportunities for:

- Beauty consultants
- Beauty therapists
- Body artists (tattooing and body piercing)
- Image consultants
- Make-up artists
- Nail technicians/manicurists
- Spa therapists
- Style analysts.

Skills and qualities needed

Anyone working in the beauty industry needs to be of smart appearance and in good health, able to apply cosmetics well, confident and friendly with a pleasant manner, able to get on well with colleagues and clients.

It also helps to have a good sales technique and some knowledge of human biology and chemistry. You may have to boost the confidence of timid or disfigured clients. Empathy, tact and consideration may be needed.

Salaries

Starting out, an Apprentice beautician would be earning the minimum wage, but with qualifications and experience can earn £11,000 yearly. A fully trained beauty therapist earns around £18,000 a year, while a manager, or someone owning their own salon, can earn £25,000 or more.

Prospects

As beauty therapy is a growing business, qualified beauty therapists can find work in salons, health clubs, hotels or on cruise ships. Many therapists are self-employed and run mobile businesses, visiting their clients at times to suit themselves.

Professional beauticians are continually upgrading their skills and knowledge and gaining manufacturers' certificates of competence and proficiency in using the latest technology. Promotion is possible by training in specialist treatments, and by moving to larger employers where there are management positions.

Consulting, advising and researching make-up and prosthetics for film, TV and theatre is at the creative edge in this field.

Ways into work

You need no formal qualifications to start in beauty work. Typically, every beauty salon and spa has up to four unfilled vacancies. You might arrange day release from school to job-shadow an employee in a salon or studio.

Trainee beauticians can enter with a few average GCSEs/ Scottish Standard grades or an NVQ/SVQ Level 1. Training as an Apprentice with an employer while following a part-time college course will allow you to gain qualified beautician status with an NVQ Level 2.

Advanced Apprenticeships can be started with a NVQ/SVQ Level 2 and lead to a technical certificate and NVQ/SVQ Level 3, when you can become a beauty therapist or manicurist, cosmetic artist or consultant, possibly running your own business.

Finding a job

For information about Apprenticeships contact your local Connexions/careers service which also holds local job opportunities for young work entrants.

Job vacancies are also advertised in local newspapers/websites and in college job centres.

CASE STUDY

Sue Over – Beautician/Salon Manager

Sue owns two beauty salons and employs 26 staff. The salons are open from 8.00a.m. to 8.00p.m. six days a week and offer a range of treatments from manicures and pedicures to hair removal, nail extensions, facials and waxing. Medical staff from a private health clinic carry out botox and collagen treatments at the salons.

By the age of 16, Sue knew she wanted to be a beauty therapist and chose to study human biology rather than biology. After the first year of an A-level course she left school to begin a two-year beauty therapy course.

Sue explains,

'At the time there were fewer beauty therapy courses than today. When I was offered a place on a course I decided to take it rather than re-apply later and risk not gaining a place.

'I knew I wanted to work for myself, so when I was trained I hired a room above a hair salon and paid the owners a percentage of my takings. My bank manager was very helpful and suggested I would do better to find premises of my own. He pointed out that they could be out of town because avoiding the congestion and parking fees in the town centre would be a bonus to clients.

'For the first few months I ran my salon alone and then took on four therapists. Soon we needed more space and I invested in a mobile van so we could carry out treatments in people's homes.

'Before too long I was looking for bigger premises, thinking that I would then close the first salon. However I realised that there was enough business for both salons and five years after the second salon opened I expanded the first to more than double its size.

'More and more people are having regular beauty treatments, which is great for business. However, as treatments become more complex, the equipment needed to carry them out becomes more expensive to buy.'

USEFUL ADDRESSES

BABTAC – British Association of Beauty Therapy and Cosmetology
Ambrose House
Meteor Court
Barnett Way
Barnwood GL4 3GG
Tel: 0845 065 9000
www.babtac.com

Freelance Hair and Beauty Federation
8 Willen Hall
Luton LU3 3XX
Tel: 01582 431783
www.fhbf.org.uk

Guild of Professional Beauty Therapists
Guild House
320 Burton Road
Derby DE23 6AF
Tel: 0845 2177383
www.beautyguild.com

HABIA – Hair and Beauty Industry Authority
Oxford House
Sixth Avenue
Sky Business Park
Robin Hood Airport
Doncaster DN9 3GG
Tel: 0845 230 6080
www.habia.org.uk

Hairdressing Council
30 Sydenham Road
Croydon CR0 2EF
Tel: 020 8760 7010
www.haircouncil.org.uk

Institute of Trichologists
Ground Floor Office
24 Langroyd Road
London SW17 7PL
Tel: 08706 070602
www.trichologists.org.uk

National Hairdressers' Federation
One Abbey Court
Fraser Road
Priory Business Park
Bedford MK44 3WH
Tel: 0845 345 6500
www.nhfuk.com

VTCT - Vocational Training Charitable Trust
Third Floor, Eastleigh House
Upper Market Street
Eastleigh
Hants SO50 9FD
Tel: 023 8068 4500
www.vtct.org.uk

World Federation of Hairdressing and Beauty Schools
PO Box 367
Coulsdon CR5 2TP
Tel: 01737 551 355
www.wfhbs.co.uk

PUBLICATIONS

Real Life Guide: Beauty Industry – 2nd edition, 2007, Trotman, £9.99

Real Life Guide: Hairdressing – 2nd edition, 2007, Trotman, £9.99

Working in Beauty and Hairdressing – 2006, DfES, downloadable from www.connexions-direct.com/winh

8 Hospitality and Catering

Today, it is not unusual for people to have two or three holiday breaks a year. As a nation, we have increased leisure time, and possibly, more available money, to spend staying in fashionable, interesting locations where we can find entertainment and eat and drink in style.

Across the UK, there is an increased trend for eating out and for eating better quality food. Business is booming across the UK in all branches of hospitality, including country inns and gastropubs, restaurants, hotels and boutique B&Bs.

With almost 50,000 new jobs being created each year, around one in seven Brits now works in this sector. There are ample opportunities for young people to start training on-the-job, and individuals with drive and commitment can develop interesting and fulfilling careers.

HOSPITALITY (FOOD, DRINK AND ACCOMMODATION)

Job opportunities

Almost 2 million people are employed in the UK hospitality and catering industry, working in fast-food outlets, pubs, restaurants, school, factory and hospital canteens, bed and breakfast accommodation, hotels, care homes and hostels.

Jobs include:

- Hotel manager
- Restaurant/catering manager
- Housekeeping manager
- Chef/cook
- Food service assistant/waiter, waitress
- Hotel receptionist
- Room attendant.

Skills and qualities needed

Tact and patience are important when dealing with the public. You may need to maintain a pleasant, cheerful face even if the pace heats up. Jobs in the hospitality industry often involve shift and weekend work, so flexibility and energy are needed. A lively but conscientious approach to the job is important. You may have to deal with the unexpected.

Salaries

Rates of pay vary greatly, both from area to area and from company to company:

- A newly trained hotel manager can earn around £24,000 a year.
- A trained restaurant manager could earn £25,000+, depending on the business and location.
- A skilled chef earns around £15,500, but pay rises with experience and increased responsibilities.
- A hotel receptionist earns around £11,000 per annum.
- Most food preparation and service assistants, bar and waiting staff and room attendants receive no more than the minimum wage.

Accommodation and food may be provided with some jobs and there may be tips which boost earnings.

Prospects

There are good prospects for promotion to management level for those who are prepared to work hard and gain work-based qualifications such as NVQs/SVQs to Levels 2 or 3. Accreditation can be gained while working full-time.

Ways into work

No formal qualifications are required to work in the hospitality industry but ensure you take a job where formal training is offered. Apprenticeships/Advanced Apprenticeships are available (see Introduction) in five areas:

- Accommodation
- Chef
- Fast food
- Restaurant
- Pub work

...leading to NVQ/SVQ Levels 2 or 3.

Schools and colleges offer the full range of hospitality and catering courses:

- **NVQ Level 1** – no entry qualifications required
- **NVQ Level 2** – entry requirements are one or two GCSEs/ Scottish Standard grades A–D/1–4
- **NVQ Level 3** in Hospitality and Catering – entry requirements are four GCSEs/Scottish Standard grades A–C/1–3.

The Institute of Hospitality (formerly, HCIMA) offers an Advanced Certificate in Hospitality Studies. Entry requirements are four GCSEs or NVQ/SVQ Level 2. Study is part time for people working in the industry.

The British Institute of Innkeeping is the professional body of the licensed retail trade. It offers a range of management qualifications, from National Licensees' Certificate and Catering Management Certificate to the Wine Retail Certificate.

Finding a job

For information about Apprenticeships contact the local Connexions/careers service which also holds local job opportunities for young work entrants.

Make a direct approach to local hospitality and catering outlets about possible job vacancies. This is often the simplest route to find paid work.

Jobs are advertised in journals such as *Caterer and Hotelkeeper* and *Catering* and in local newspapers/web pages.

CASE STUDY

Ben Handley

An appreciation of good food runs in Ben's family. His parents used to run the Lifeboat Inn at Thornham on the Norfolk coast. After GCSEs Ben joined them and worked in the kitchen for four years learning his trade. He also went to Norfolk City College on day release for the City & Guilds 7061 and 7062 courses and gained an NVQ in Catering.

At 19 Ben decided to gain further experience and did relief work around the country before going to Titchwell Manor in Norfolk as sous chef and then as head chef. When wanderlust got the better of him, he set off for Australia and spent several months working in a restaurant in Melbourne. He says:

'I loved the blending of different food cultures – Thai, Chinese, Italian, French.'

Ben is now head chef at the White Horse in Brancaster Staithe on the North Norfolk coast. It is a job that gives him ample opportunity to experiment with Mediterranean-type fish dishes, which he loves.

In his words,

'You're always learning and experimenting when you're a chef, which is great. Eventually, when I've learned enough, I'd like to open my own restaurant.'

USEFUL ADDRESSES

Hospitality

The British Institute of Innkeeping
Wessex House
80 Park Street
Camberley GU15 3PT
Tel: 01276 684449
www.bii.org

Institute of Hospitality (formerly HCIMA)
Trinity Court
34 West Street
Sutton SM1 1SH
Tel: 020 8661 4900
www.hcima.org.uk

People 1st
Sector Skills Council for the Hospitality, Leisure, Travel and
Tourism Industries
2nd Floor, Armstrong House
38 Market Square
Uxbridge UB8 1LH
Tel: 0870 060 2550
www.people1st.co.uk

PUBLICATIONS

Real Life Guide: Catering – 2nd edition, 2007, Trotman,
   £9.99
Working in Food and Drink – 2006, VT Lifeskills, £8.50

9   Leisure, Sport and Tourism

SPORT AND LEISURE

Sport and recreation are great ways to relax and unwind and there are ongoing government initiatives which encourage people to lead healthier lifestyles. There is no age limit to physical activities. Children from around age two enjoy pre-school play and exercise groups, while many retired people belong to golf and swimming clubs or take keep-fit and yoga classes.

Very few people reach professional status in a particular sport. The vast majority are simply enthusiastic amateurs who enjoy themselves, whatever the standard they achieve, and who value the chance to get out, keep fit and meet people.

Job opportunities

Careers in the sport and leisure industry can be followed in:

- Sport and recreation – leisure centres, stadiums and arenas, sports clubs, professional sport, development and administration
- Health and fitness – health and leisure clubs, gyms, fitness suites in hotels and holiday complexes
- The outdoors – outdoor pursuit centres, water sports centres, ski resorts
- Children's play – out-of-school clubs, adventure playgrounds, play buses
- Leisure parks and attractions.

Skills and qualities

Energy and enthusiasm are important, and so is an interest in sport at every level, plus the ability to motivate people of all ages! You have to be able to work as part of a team where, sometimes, you might take the lead. Clear communication skills, both spoken and written, are important. A mature, consistent and responsible attitude to health and safety matters is of critical importance.

Salaries

A leisure centre attendant earns in the region of £10,000 to £12,000 per annum. Fitness instructors can earn from £11,000 per annum while qualified, specialist instructors earn higher salaries, from £16,000 to over £24,000 annually.

Depending on areas of responsibility, experience, centre size and location, an outdoor activities instructor may earn from £9,000 to over £22,000 annually. Lifeguards can earn £10,000–£12,000 per annum.

Prospects

There are good opportunities for promotion to supervisory and management levels. It is considered important for all entrants to gain experience at a day-to-day working level in a leisure or fitness centre, before moving to senior positions.

Ways into work

There are both vocational and academic routes into sport and leisure including GCSE/Scottish Standard qualifications in Physical Education (and Applied Leisure and Tourism which can be useful for leisure centre work). A 14–19 specialist Diploma in Retail, Sport and Leisure will not be available until 2010. AS-or A-levels are available in Sport and Physical Education, Leisure and Recreation which can lead to job opportunities. Practical qualifications in First Aid or Lifeguarding are also helpful when looking for a job. Apprenticeships leading to an NVQ/SVQ Level 2 or 3 are available (see Introduction). There are NVQs/ SVQs in Sport and Recreation from Levels 1 to 4.

Finding a job

For information about Apprenticeships contact your local Connexions/careers service which also holds local job opportunities. One common route into full-time work is through part-time or voluntary work with an organisation. Details of centres approved to deliver NVQs/SVQs can be found on the SkillsActive website (see Useful addresses).

TRAVEL AND TOURISM

Travel and tourism employs 1.6 million people and is the UK's fastest growing industry.

Visitors from abroad are drawn to the UK by its varied scenery and historical buildings and traditions. A growing number of British people take short breaks in other parts of the country, in cities such as London, York and Edinburgh and in scenic areas such as the Lake District, Cornwall or the Scottish Highlands. As well as taking breaks in this country more people than ever are leaving the UK for holidays in places such as Spain, France and Greece and further afield in the Far East and the US.

Job opportunities

Leisure travel agent or consultant

This is work in a travel agency, finding out what customers want, advising on resorts and travel arrangements, selling airline tickets, arranging car hire, booking holidays using a computerised system, advising on visas, inoculations, insurance, foreign currency.

Courier/resort representative

A 'rep' makes sure all runs smoothly and that visitors enjoy their holiday. They either travel with holidaymakers or greet them at their holiday destination. They answer enquiries, give information about the resort, organise trips and activities and deal with emergencies such as lost luggage or illness.

Skills and qualities needed

Both travel agents and couriers/resort representatives need to be sociable and like working with people. Tact and patience are essential and so is quick thinking and having a smart professional appearance.

Holiday bookings are done by computer, so IT skills for agents and consultants are important, as is a good standard of writing and numerical skills.

Not all couriers/resort representatives speak the language of the country they are working in, but fluency in a foreign language is a great asset.

Salaries

A trained travel consultant can earn between £154 and £250 a week. An experienced travel consultant dealing in a specialised area such as business travel can earn up to £307 a week. Travel consultants usually get discounts on their own holidays. A courier/resort representative usually receives free accommodation and meals and earns between £90 and £190 a week, depending on experience.

Prospects

Most couriers or representatives work short-term on a fixed contract for a season, although the growing popularity of winter holiday destinations means there are some opportunities for working all year round. Most people spend a few seasons working as couriers/resort representatives and then move on to other work. With large travel companies there are openings for tour managers and courier supervisors.

For travel consultants working with large companies there are good promotion opportunities to manager and area manager and openings in tourist information centres.

Ways into work

Travel agent/consultant

A good standard of education is needed and some employers ask particularly for GCSE grades A–C, Scottish Standard grades 1–3 in English and Maths.

Most young people go into the work through the Modern Apprenticeship programmes, which lead to an NVQ/SVQ Levels 2 or 3 and Key Skills (see Introduction). There are NVQs/

SVQs Levels 2, 3 and 4 and many large companies run their own training programmes.

There are also BTEC/SQA Higher National Certificates and Diploma courses in travel and tourism. Entry requirements are one or two A-level or Scottish Higher grades, plus GCSE A–C grades/Scottish Standard grades 1–3 or equivalent qualifications.

Courier/resort representative

Couriers need to be over the age of 18. Companies look for people who have experience working with the public and abroad. Some ask for GCSEs/Scottish Standard grades A–C/1–3 in English, and Maths. Knowledge of a foreign language, even without a formal qualification, is a good selling point.

Some couriers/resort representatives take a travel and tourism qualification and the Apprenticeship programme is used by the larger companies (see under Travel agent/consultant). Companies run induction courses to prepare couriers/resort representatives for the work – covering problems they are likely to meet. Couriers can work towards NVQs/SVQs at Levels 2 and 3 in Travel Services.

Finding a job

To apply for a job as a travel courier/resort representative, contact travel companies at least six months in advance of the season. These jobs are very popular and companies don't need to advertise. When they do they use national newspapers and trade publications such as *Overseas Jobs Express*, and *Travel Weekly*.

For information about Apprenticeships contact the local Connexions/careers service which holds local job opportunities for young work entrants.

CASE STUDY

Sarah Chapman

Sarah, 26, is assistant manager of a travel agency.

'I left school after GCSEs and took an NVQ Level 2 in Business Administration at the local college. When I finished the training I found a job in a travel agency and thoroughly enjoyed it.

'During the next five years with the company I gained an NVQ at Levels 2 and 3 in Travel and Tourism. My next job was assistant manager with a larger agency, and that's where I am now.

'When the manager is absent I am responsible for running the agency, looking after the administration and checking all is well with staff and customers. I'm qualified to work in the foreign exchange section and I also dress the windows, making sure the information is up to date and attractive.

'We're busy throughout the year, but our most hectic times are January and February when people are tired of the winter and want to look forward to a break in the sun. July and August are also busy when those who haven't booked a holiday want a last-minute bargain. Some people take brochures away and work out for themselves what they want. But many of them need help to find their dream holiday. Staff also organise tailor-made holidays for customers who want to plan their own holiday route, possibly travelling across several countries, and they need us to organise hotels and flights for them.

'At present, I'm working towards my NVQ Level 4 through day release. This qualification covers management practices.

'To enjoy my job you need to be able to put people at their ease, chatting to them and being enthusiastic about their plans. Hours are long in the travel industry. I work most weekends and we open on Sunday at peak times. The pay isn't amazing but there are perks. I've just returned from a week's educational cruise and staff do have discounted holidays.'

USEFUL ADDRESSES

Sport and leisure

ISPAL – The Institute for Sports, Parks and Leisure
The Grotto House
Lower Basildon
Reading RG8 9NE
Tel: 0845 603 8734
www.ispal.org.uk

People 1st
Sector Skills Council for the Hospitality, Leisure, Travel
and Tourism Industries
2nd Floor, Armstrong House
38 Market Square
Uxbridge UB8 1LH
Tel: 0870 060 2550
www.people1st.co.uk

SkillsActive – Sector Skills Council for Active Leisure
and Learning
Castlewood House
77–91 New Oxford Street
London WC1A 1PX
Tel: 020 7632 2000
www.skillsactive.com

Sports Coach UK
114 Cardigan Road
Headingley
Leeds LS6 3BJ
Tel: 0113 274 4802
www.sportscoachuk.org

Travel and tourism

Springboard UK
3 Denmark Street
London WC2H 8LP
Tel: 020 7497 8654
www.springboarduk.org.uk

PUBLICATIONS

Real Life Guide: Travel and Tourism – 2nd edition, 2008,
Trotman, £9.99
Sport and Fitness Uncovered – 2006, Trotman, £11.99
Travel Industry Uncovered – 2006, Trotman, £11.99
Working in Sport and Fitness – 2006, DfES, downloadable
from www.connexions-direct.com/win
Working in Travel and Tourism – 2006, DfES, downloadable
from www.connexions-direct.com/win

10 Medical, Healthcare, Social Care

Recently, due to high immigration and rising birth rates, there has been a sharp upturn in Britain's population. By 2020, there will be more than 62 million of us, all requiring healthcare and support at different stages of our lives. With increasing longevity and many more over-65s, there is already a growing need for health and social care workers.

You can start in health and care-related work with four or five GCSEs/Scottish Standard grades, but there are opportunities for more rapid progression and career development if you have two to three A-levels/Scottish Higher qualifications.

HEALTHCARE WORK

Although many nurses now train through a nursing degree course, there are still opportunities for those with four to five GCSEs/Scottish Standard grades at A–C/1–3 (including Maths, English and Science) to start as healthcare assistants and train for a Nursing Diploma. You can gain qualifications in work with part-time study or, through a full-time course.

Job opportunities

The National Health Service is the largest employer of healthcare assistants and nurses. With continuing and increasing healthcare need, employment prospects are excellent.

Healthcare assistants and nurses work in a variety of settings including GP practice surgeries, hospital wards and outpatient clinics, hospices, walk-in health centres, care homes, patients' homes, schools and factories. Some nurses obtain work through nursing agencies.

Trained nurses can find paid or volunteer work anywhere in the world, particularly in countries that are war-torn or dealing with crises.

Skills and qualities needed

Nurses have to get on well with people of all ages and backgrounds. They need to be reliable and conscientious, with a high level of sensitivity, tact and understanding, well organised, practical and able to remain calm in an emergency or a crisis. Usually working as part of a team, nurses also undertake tasks alone.

Salaries

The starting salary for an unqualified nurse in the NHS is around £16,500 per annum. Qualified registered nurses earn from £18,700 and, with experience, over £35,500. Nurses in the highest paid posts (as nurse consultants) can earn £45,000.

Prospects

Employment prospects are very good. As well as working in the NHS, nurses are employed in private hospitals and clinics, nursing or care homes and in industry. There are opportunities for experienced nurses to move into management nursing posts, or to go into research or education, some, working as consultants. Nurses specialise in mental health, learning disability, adult or child nursing. Being a fully trained nurse opens routes into further specialisation, for example, as a midwife, district or community nurse, or health visitor.

Ways into work

There are a number of ways to enter nurse training:

- People starting as healthcare assistants in the NHS can take NVQs/SVQs in Care at Levels 2 and 3. Level 3 is accepted as the minimum educational requirement for entry to a nursing Diploma programme.
- From September 2008, 14–19 specialised Diploma courses in Health and Social Care will be available across schools and colleges.
- Access to Nursing courses are available for people over 19 years without traditional entry requirements for

either nursing or midwifery. These courses must be Quality Assurance Agency (QAA) approved. Successful completion of the course meets the entry requirements for both the Nursing Diploma and degree programmes.

- Foundation degree completion will now allow a person to enter the second year of either the Diploma (or degree) nursing programme.

Students need to be aged 17 years and six months or over to start training on the Diploma course. Entry qualifications are five GCSEs/Scottish Standard grades A–C/1–3 (English is required in Scotland) or an equivalent qualification such as NVQ/SVQ Level 3 or an A-level in Applied Health and Social Care. Diploma courses last for three years.

Students undertaking a Diploma course choose one of four branches of nursing – adult, child, mental health or learning disability – each requiring different aptitudes, skills and interests. There is considerable competition for entry to some branches of nursing and applicants should check the situation with each higher education institution before applying.

Most student nurses receive financial support in the form of National Health Service bursaries during their training.

Finding a job

During the second part of Diploma training, students are on practical placements in a variety of healthcare settings where they learn about job opportunities. There is heavy demand for trained nurses in all areas of the country. Jobs are advertised in *The Nursing Standard* and *The Nursing Times*. Many employers advertise job vacancies on their own websites.

CASE STUDY

Ben Bowers

Ben, who is dyslexic, left school with no qualifications and no ideas about a career. He went to college and took GCSEs in English, Maths and Business Studies and decided to go into retail.

In his words,

'For the next five years my one ambition was to have enough
money to enjoy myself with my friends.'

As he got older Ben began to give his future some thought and
wondered about joining the police. He became a special constable
(voluntary policeman) in his spare time and, through his work,
sometimes found himself inside a hospital. The more he saw of hospital work, the more Ben liked the concept. He eventually, took a job
as a nursing auxiliary (healthcare assistant).

'Originally, I thought I would gain the qualifications to train
as a nurse through my work, but I realised this would take a
long time, so I went back to college and took a year-long Access
course studying psychology, sociology and human biology.

'I'm now 24 and in my second year of training in a
Cambridge hospital, working towards the Registered Nursing
Diploma. The course is half practical, half theory. I find nursing exciting and stimulating, though not without its difficult
moments. My ambition is to specialise in neurology, dealing
with problems affecting the central nervous system.'

CASE STUDY

Eve Almond

Eve is a student nurse working for her Diploma in Nursing and
specialising in mental health. She chose mental health nursing because she feels it offers a chance to form a closer caring relationship
with patients than other types of nursing. Mental health nursing
includes working in hospital and in the community, looking after
patients of all ages including those with acute or serious illnesses and
those with long-term problems.

Now in her final year, Eve is specialising in work with adolescents and her long-term plan is to do therapeutic work with young
people.

It took Eve some time to discover that she wanted to take up nursing as a career. She explains,

'I started an A-level course because I was quite good at graphics. I wasn't really interested in the course and dropped out
after a year. To be honest I'm not sure the school noticed I'd
gone.

'My mother was a healthcare assistant in a hospital and I joined her there because it was a convenient job and I wanted to save money and travel. I enjoyed the work and began to think seriously about nursing.

'I took four months off and travelled around the world, then came back and applied for a training place as a nurse in Brighton. Once I'd gained a place I went off again, this time to Canada where I worked as a volunteer on farming projects.

'It took me quite a while to adjust to the training course. After nine weeks of theory in the classroom, we were on the ward for ten weeks' nursing practice. The course is tough and it isn't for anyone who isn't committed to nursing. I have enjoyed it and I'm looking forward to a career working closely with young people.'

DENTAL CARE

Many people, understanding the psychological importance of smiling and the nutritional difficulties and problems that can arise for those with poor dentition, are keen to gain the knowledge and skills to help young and older dental patients.

Job opportunities

Dental nurse

This job involves looking after and tending to patients, preparing equipment, mixing materials such as fillings, updating records, sterilising instruments and, sometimes, acting as a dental receptionist.

Dental technician

Dental technicians make up dental appliances such as braces, crowns, bridges and dentures from prescriptions written by dentists.

Skills and qualities needed

Dental nurses

Dental nurses need to have a calm friendly manner and an understanding approach towards patients – including the ones who are tense and nervous. You must have good communication skills, close attention to hygiene, a neat professional appearance and the ability to cope with difficult situations. An interest in biology is also important.

Dental technicians

Dental technicians need a sharp eye for detail. You should be dextrous with excellent hand-eye coordination and have an interest in science and technology as you will need to keep up with continuing developments. Good communication skills and the ability to work with others are important.

Salaries

A trained registered dental nurse earns around £14,500 a year, rising to around £19,000 with experience.

Dental technicians earn a minimum annual salary of £17,000 when qualified. In positions of responsibility, earnings can reach £30,000+ per annum.

Prospects

In dental hospitals and dental centres there are opportunities for dental nurses to reach senior positions. They can take further training in oral health education, dental anaesthetic nursing or become a hygienist. In hospitals or large dental practices there are management opportunities for dental nurses.

There is a promotional ladder for technicians leading to the position of chief dental technician in charge of a laboratory. In the commercial sector dental technicians can work at all levels and become self-employed.

Ways into work

Dental nurse

Many dentists are willing to train dental nurses without formal entry requirements, although GCSE/Scottish Standard grades in English and Double Science are helpful. Nurses training this way should study for the National Certificate for Dental Nurses run by many colleges as a part-time evening course.

There are also full-time one or two-year training courses run by colleges and hospitals. Entry requirements for these are usually two to four GCSEs/Scottish Standard grades A–C/1–3, preferably including English language and Double Science. NVQs/SVQs at Level 2 and 3 are available in Oral Healthcare Support.

Dental technician

The essential qualification for a dental technician to be able to register to practice with the General Dental Council is a BTEC/SQA National Diploma in Dental Technology. Entry requirements are four GCSE/Scottish Standard grades at A–C/1–3 to include Science and possibly Maths, a BTEC First Certificate in Science or equivalent qualification.

There are four main training routes:

- A training place within a commercial laboratory whilst attending a further education college course one day a week for up to five years
- A two-year full-time course in dental technology
- A four year sandwich course within the NHS, where part of the time is spent at college and part in the laboratory
- A full-time two-year Foundation degree requiring the equivalent of one A-level/Scottish Higher for entry.

Finding a job

Careers information is available from professional bodies (see under Useful addresses) and from Connexions/careers offices. Job vacancies are often advertised in the local press/websites and in *The Dental Technician* and *British Dental Nurses' Journal*.

OPHTHALMICS

Having a job where you assist optometrists in the correction of people's eyesight – and so improve their quality of life – can be highly rewarding! Optometrists rely on ophthalmic specialists to correctly dispense the lenses they have diagnosed and prescribed, made up either as contact lenses or framed spectacles, to suit.

Job opportunities

As a dispensing optician, you would order prescriptions for spectacles and contact lenses from manufacturers, measure patients and fit spectacles and contact lenses, advising on style and types of spectacles.

Skills and qualities needed

Interest in science and the ability to handle scientific instruments are necessary, as are patience and good communication skills. An interest in fashion is important as glasses are now a fashion item for many people.

Salaries

A trained dispensing optician can earn between £15,000 and £25,000 a year.

Prospects

There are good opportunities for promotion to management level and for specialisation. Some highly experienced ophthalmic opticians run their own businesses. Dispensing opticians who go on to train as optometrists are exempt from certain parts of the course.

Ways into work

Dispensing opticians must pass the professional examinations of the Association of British Dispensing Opticians (ABDO). Entry requirements are five GCSEs/Scottish Standard grades A–C/1–4 including English, Maths and a science. An Access course is run by ABDO for candidates over 19 years who do not have the usual entry requirements. Full- and part-time

Diploma courses are run at Anglia Polytechnic University and City College Islington.

Finding a job

Most dispensing opticians work in ophthalmic practices, which range from small independent businesses to national chains, although some are employed in the eye departments of hospitals. Jobs may be advertised locally or in professional journals such as *Dispensing Optics*.

PHARMACY

Pharmacy is concerned with the preparation and dispensing of prescribed medicines for patients. The work of a pharmacy technician is usually carried out under the supervision of a qualified pharmacist.

Job opportunities

Pharmacy technicians work in chemist's shops, practice or community pharmacies, and in hospital pharmacy departments.

Community pharmacy technicians help pharmacists by assembling items listed on prescriptions, checking that the products match those on the list and labelling drugs with details of name, strength and dosage instructions. They keep records and check stock levels, ordering supplies whenever necessary.

Hospital pharmacy technicians work in a team under a hospital pharmacist. They dispense drugs, check supplies and place orders with pharmaceutical companies.

Industrial pharmacy technicians work in laboratories, assisting pharmacists in specialised areas such as research or clinical trials.

Skills and qualities needed

Pharmacy technicians need a high level of interest in medicine and science; also, the ability to work methodically and accurately, paying close attention to detail. They should be numerate, as well as clear communicators who enjoy working as part of a team. Pharmacy technicians dealing directly with patients or customers need to be friendly, patient and sympathetic.

Salaries

Rates of pay vary greatly depending on the location and size of the company. The average salary of a pharmacy technician is between £12,000 and £14,000 a year, rising to around £16,500 after a few years' experience. Those who gain management-level responsibilities in hospital pharmacies can earn up to £38,000.

Prospects

There are good promotion prospects for pharmacy technicians in hospitals, where large departments have opportunities for taking on management responsibilities and for specialisation. There is also a growing demand for pharmacy technicians in the community as supermarkets open dispensing counters.

Pharmacy technicians cannot become pharmacists without going to university, taking a four-year pharmacy degree course and completing a one-year period of pre-registration training.

Ways into work

No formal qualifications are necessary but it is helpful to have studied science to GCSE/Scottish Standard level. Hospitals often look for four GCSEs A–C grades/Scottish Standard grades 1–3 including English, Science and Maths.

The NVQ/SVQ Level 3 in Pharmacy Services is the principal qualification for pharmacy technicians. This qualification demands a great deal of underpinning knowledge as well as the usual NVQ requirements, and most trainees achieve this knowledge through studying for the BTEC/SQA Certificate in Pharmaceutical Studies.

Most pharmacy technicians train while on the job. Community technicians tend to train by distance learning and those in hospitals, through day release. The BTEC/SQA course takes from two to three years on a day-release basis and can lead to entry to a Higher National course.

An Advanced Apprenticeship (see Introduction) is available.

Finding a job

Information concerning Apprenticeships is available from your local Connexions/careers service which can also give advice on pharmacy technician careers and job opportunities locally.

Jobs are also advertised in the local press and in *The Chemist and Druggist* and *The Pharmacy Journal*.

SOCIAL CARE

Here, you need to have an interest in caring for the elderly or for those with disabilities who cannot live independently. Some jobs involve looking after people in residential care, in other posts you work in the community, visiting individuals in sheltered accommodation or in their own home. There are well over one million care assistants practising in the UK, and the need for this work is rising.

Skills and qualities needed

You need to be 18 to work as a care assistant. Care work needs patience, coupled with a strong sense of empathy and compassion. It can be wearing, helping individuals who cannot always verbalise their needs, so you need to be cheerful with a well-developed sense of humour, practical and methodical, and good at working in a team.

The work suits those who get a strong sense of satisfaction from assisting individuals to improve their quality of life. People who become social care workers sometimes are, or have been, carers themselves.

Salaries and prospects

Pay is at just above the minimum wage for those aged 18, but rises with experience and qualifications in Care. With

NVQ/SVQ at Level 3, you can take n more responsibilities and move towards supervisory jobs, preparing for management-level posts where pay can approach £21,000. There is overtime pay for night and weekend duties.

Ways into work

Many young people take courses at school or college in Health and Social Care at GCSE/Scottish Standard grade and as an Applied A-level. This training involves work experience on a placement, and many individuals decide then, whether the work suits them in the longer term.

There are also BTEC/SQA First and National qualifications in Health and Social Care available through college courses.

You can work in care homes for the elderly or young people with special needs as an Apprentice, training and qualifying through NVQs/SVQs in Care to Levels 2 and 3.

Finding a job

Information and help with starting an Apprenticeship is held by your local Connexions/careers service, where you can get advice on training for a career in the work.

The simplest route to finding work is by word of mouth; almost every residential care home will recruit care assistants during the course of a year. Jobs are advertised in the job centre or local paper.

USEFUL ADDRESSES

Dental care

British Association of Dental Nurses
PO Box 4
Room 7, Hillhouse International Business Centre
Thornton-Cleveleys FY5 4QD
Tel: 0870 211 0113
www.badn.org.uk

British Dental Hygienists' Association
Mobbs Miller House
Ardington Road
Northampton NN1 5LP
Email: enquiries@bdha.org.uk
www.bdha.org.uk

DTA – British Technologists' Association
PO Box 6520
Northampton NN3 9ZX
Tel: 0870 243 0753
www.dta-uk.org

Nursing

Careers Advice
School of Nursing and Midwifery
Medical Biology Centre
Queen's University Belfast
97 Lisburn Road
Belfast BT9 7BL
Tel: 028 9097 2233
www.qub.ac.uk/schools/

NHS Careers
PO Box 2311
Bristol BS2 2ZX
Tel: 0845 6060 655
www.nhs.uk/careers
www.jobs.nhs.uk

NHS: National Services Scotland
Gyle Square
1 South Gyle Crescent
Edinburgh EH12 9EB
Tel: 0131 275 6000
www.nhsnss.org

Royal College of Midwives
15 Mansfield Street
London W1G 9NH
Tel: 020 7312 3535
www.rcm.org.uk

Royal College of Nursing
20 Cavendish Square
London W1G 0RN
Tel: 020 7409 3333
www.rcn.org.uk

Ophthalmics

ABDO– Association of British Dispensing Opticians
College of Education
Godmersham Park
Godmersham CT4 7DT
Tel: 01227 738829
www.abdo.org.uk

Pharmacy technician

The National Pharmacy Association
Mallinson House
38–42 St Peter's Street
St Albans AL1 3NP
Tel: 01727 832161
www.npa.co.uk

Social care

Skills for Care and Development – the Sector Skills Council
Albion Court
5 Albion Place
Leeds LS1 6JL
Tel: 0113 245 1716
www.skillsforcare.org.uk

PUBLICATIONS

Directory of Nursing and Midwifery Courses – 2004, Trotman, £15.99

Working in Hospitals; Working in Community Healthcare; Working in Social Care – 2006, VT Lifeskills at £8.50 each

11 Performing Arts

You may have watched many a talent show such as *American Pop Idol*, the *X Factor* or *Any Dream Will Do* and thought – 'I could do that, and do it better!' Everyone has a talent or skill that they enjoy practising. Many individuals would be thrilled to develop that skill into paid work and a career, preferably where they also become famous and wealthy! Some young people do live their dream and manage to support themselves practising performing arts; some, through working on set and many more through supporting operations behind the scenes.

Across the UK there are 1,500 performing arts companies receiving a variable proportion of public support through Arts Council grants, but many more companies rely on local and private funding alone. Of 200 dance companies, only a small number receive regular grants to ensure their economic survival. It is a frail industry in terms of long-term expectations and career projections – but, that's entertainment for you!

Job opportunities

These arise in large companies running theatres, film, video and TV studios, ballet, opera and concert halls, music and entertainment venues including holiday camps, and cruise ships, as well as circuses. Many openings are within small, even microfirms. To work your way up to earning a living as a top-level performer takes more than being talented, and very few people achieve continuous employment as actors, singers, dancers, violinists, guitar players, puppeteers, story tellers, clowns, mime artists or acrobats.

Not everyone wants to be in the frame or the spotlights. Many enjoy working in supportive functions to the performing roles. You might work on the design and build of sets; researching, designing and making costumes; planning the lighting for a production; working as part of the stage management crew or as riggers, lighting and sound engineers – even, playing music in rehearsals or in the orchestra pit rather than on stage as a virtuoso.

CASE STUDY

Oli Porteous – DJ, Techno Dance Music Composer

Interested in all kinds of sounds, Oli played drums and keyboard outside school, but had chosen to study A-levels in Maths, Physics and Art and Design. He had done a spell of work experience in a local architect's office and thought he might go that route at university.

Sometimes, Oli spent too much time using the school's drum kit when he should have been studying. Also, keeping ahead with the latest techno music occupied time at home and at gigs. In Oli's words,

'It became obvious that I wasn't making progress with my A-levels. I found the Maths hard work and didn't spend enough time getting the extra help I needed. Music had become my whole life and I gambled on making it my career.

'I transferred to a BTEC National Diploma course in Popular Music at the local college where, for the first time, I couldn't wait to crack on with work. Every minute was dedicated to talking about, listening to, analysing and trying to emulate a range of music genres. I played all the instruments I could get my hands on and tried live performance as a drummer with several bands.

'I learned to do my own compositions using AudioLogic software and this gave me the biggest thrill. I tried out my own sounds at festi's in the South West over the next two years, and gradually got my name known for techno. Clubs around the Bristol area started inviting me as guest, then resident DJ.

'It's tough staying up all night to play a 3am slot and then get on with college assignments, but I made the qualification! And, I scored distinction for film score music.

'Now, I have a recording contract to produce a number of dance tunes each year, but I make most money through occasional appearances as a techno DJ.

'I've joined forces with two like-minded individuals who understand everything about sound equipment and we've set up a recording studio where I help bands mix their sounds and produce MP3s. We also build and deliver customised sound systems and I supply vinyl to other DJs through our Bristol outlet. I need the regular income of this growing business. There's no surviving solely on DJ performances. Few make it to the top of the tree and there's only a little time on the best perch!

'I can truly say I've no regrets about not doing a degree course. Actually, I've not had the time. I'm just starting to write music for film!'

Skills and qualities needed

To reach recognition as a performer, besides a high level of talent and physical fitness, you need a sizeable amount of self-belief and confidence in your own abilities. Live or videoed performance is not a career area for the faint-hearted, shy individual. You need to be thick-skinned and not mind rebuffs and set-backs as every performer will meet these throughout their career – the good, as well as the not – so-good.

Performers need to be reliable time-keepers, with a well-developed sense of responsibility and concern for the success of the whole production, performance, musical show or gig. Other artists will be relying on you to play your part.

It helps to have a good memory as there are routines, lines or sequences to recall. You need clear communication skills, the ability to work well with others and, importantly, a good sense of humour.

Actors, singers, mime artists and dancers need creative and interpretative skills which require a high degree of emotional intelligence. Patience will be required, as there will be long waits during rehearsals, between performances and between jobs.

Salaries

Unless you make it to the top of your chosen profession, you can expect to earn about £15,000 per annum when fully employed. Most performers are part-time and earn considerably less. Those working in support roles to performers, who have permanent jobs in theatres, concert halls or with individual companies, can expect to start at around £10,000 per annum, rising to about £19,500 with qualifications to Level 3 and some years of experience. Stage, theatre and company managers earn rather more; while TV and film producers and directors start around £17,000 per annum but can earn considerable sums, some being in a position to select jobs and agree their own salary.

Prospects

There is a degree of luck in the career of any performing artist, for example being seen/heard at an appropriate moment to make an impression, having the physical attributes needed for a role, being able to attend auditions, etc. Many actors and dancers have agents who act as scouts, finding roles for performers on their books.

You may spend your working life in the cello section of a well-known orchestra which has bookings throughout the year, in this country and abroad. A part in a prominent play might develop into a film role which could lead to a long fulfilling and highly acclaimed career. The other extreme is that you may be asked to do only a couple of DJ sessions in a six-month period.

Some performing arts ventures are liable to collapse through lack of funding or lack of private support. Besides maintaining a degree of optimism, the best advice is to stay fit and in shape through continued training, but have a second career string to your bow!

Ways into work

People who enjoy performing arts have usually taken part in productions, music concerts or gigs, both inside and outside school. They may have gained work experience with amateur groups during summer holidays and even stood in as a player or part of the wardrobe team, or joined the rigging, stage or lighting crew. Hands-on experience can stand you in good stead when you're seeking paid work.

There are GCSEs/Scottish Standard grades in Performing Arts and Dance, as well as a single award Applied A-level.

Many students take National Diploma qualifications in Performing Arts.

A new initiative by the Cultural and Creative Skills Sector is to offer Creative Apprenticeships for young school-leavers keen to train in specialist pathways for live events and promotion, music business (recording industry), technology and theatre (rigging, lighting and sound), costume and wardrobe, cultural venue operations and community arts. If you can find a job with an enterprise which would allow you to learn as you earn, taking an Apprenticeship could lead to Level 3 qualifications in the industry, and open wider opportunities.

Young dancers, choreographers and actors usually train through a vocational course offered by a specialist college that can demand five GCSEs/Scottish Standard grades A–C/1–3 at entry. You have to audition and your level of physical fitness will be assessed. Colleges award their own Diploma, Professional Diploma, National Diploma and even degree-level qualifications.

Popular or creative music courses, with training in ensemble playing and live performance, are offered at colleges across the UK and lead to BTEC National Diplomas in Music Technology, Audio Technology or Performance. These courses require four or five GCSEs/Scottish Standard grades for entry. Some take these qualifications higher, obtaining Foundation degrees in their specialism.

Completers of National Council for Drama Training or Circus Arts courses are entitled to become members of Equity – the Trade Union in Performing Arts for UK residents – and so are licensed to work in this country.

Finding a job

Once a member of Equity, you can use their jobs vacancies listings; but there are many publications advertising work opportunities: *The Stage, Spotlight, Sound on Sound* etc. 17% of companies in this industrial sector are seeking skilled employees.

Useful addresses

CCSkills – Creative and Cultural Sector Skills Council
4th Floor, Lafone House
The Leathermarket
Weston Street
London SE1 3HN
Tel: 020 7015 1847
www.ccskills.org.uk

Equity
Head Office
Guild House
Upper St Martin's Lane
London WC2H 9EG
Tel: 020 7379 6000
www.equity.org.uk

Other useful websites

www.spotlightcd.com
www.thestage.com/recruitment/

Publications

Working in Performing Arts; Working in Music – 2006, VT
  Lifeskills at £8.50
Performing Arts Uncovered – 2nd edition, 2007, Trotman,
  £12.99

12 Retail and Customer Services

RETAIL

Retail operations vary from small, family owned shops and market stalls to national organisations such as Waitrose or Debenhams and global operations such as Tesco and The Body Shop. Of course, you no longer need a shop front to run a retail operation. Mail order or e-retail companies offer a home delivery service to customers who buy products online via websites.

Job opportunities

These include the following:

- Retail assistant
- Checkout assistant or till operator
- Shelf-filler/replenishment assistant
- Department manager/store manager
- Display/visual merchandiser.

CASE STUDY

Jamie McClellan – Retail Manager: Wines and Spirits, Marks & Spencer

'I did go to uni, but couldn't take the impersonal lectures in a vast theatre where Business Studies seemed to bear no relation to real life, nor to business in the raw. I got dispirited and dropped out after a year in campus.

'I knew a fair amount about the retail business as I'd had a part-time job with M&S since Year 12, so I went back there in the summer and they took me on full-time that autumn. I was moved from shelf replenishment into Customer Service where I dealt with returns after the following Christmas!

'I now have an NVQ Level 3 in Customer Services, having thoroughly tested my training in communication skills and building confidence in the stores' service with many hundreds of mildly dissatisfied customers.

'My big break came the following spring when the wine buyer was retiring and I work shadowed him for three months, finding out about the products and their sourcing. I now had to learn a whole new vocabulary to describe the wines which M&S select. I've been encouraged to take the fast-track management training scheme and have been to several training days at M&S Headquarters where, besides a host of other things, we learn all about expedient purchasing of vintages. We also get to taste the wines and make qualified remarks on their 'nose'.

'Back on the shop floor, I find that my understanding of how the business operates is much more comprehensive – also fascinating because I'm learning on-the-job. I can see at first-hand which bottles fly off the shelves and I'm always ready to pick up customer feedback.

'My efforts are bringing their own rewards, management responsibility and a good wage, and I *do* love my job!'

Skills and qualities needed

Retail assistants have to know the products they are selling so they can talk to customers about them. Patience, a friendly manner and a sense of humour are essential.

Managers also need to be highly knowledgeable about products on sale but, as well as qualities which help them to get on well with customers and employees, they have to motivate staff, make quick decisions and take control when necessary. Good organisational skills and business awareness are important.

Visual merchandisers arrange attractive window and in-store displays to stimulate the customers to buy goods. To do this job, they need artistic flair and a well-developed sense of colour and design. As a visual merchandiser, you have to be prepared to work as part of a team and, as you will be frequently meeting customers, politeness and a friendly manner are also important.

Salaries

Replenishment assistants and sales assistants usually earn £9,000–£10,000 per year, checkout assistants around £11,000 and department supervisors or managers between £18,000 and £40,000, depending on the scale of the business. Senior managers in large stores can earn more than £60,000 annually. Visual merchandisers earn around £11,000 per annum, starting out. Most stores provide staff with benefits such as discounts.

Prospects

Larger stores offer promising retail assistants opportunities for promotion to senior sales posts and to supervisory or management positions. Some companies run their own management training programmes and many store managers began their careers as assistants. In turn, retail managers can progress to area or regional management or head office positions. There are good work opportunities for visual merchandisers with recognised qualifications in shops, airports, cruise liners, museums, libraries, pubs, exhibition display and with local authorities.

Ways into work

Information on the industry can be found on Skillsmart's website www.skillsmart.com which also provides online advice and guidance.

Skillsmart produces a twice-yearly publication, *Retail Therapy*, which is available free to all young people. The Institute of Grocery Distribution has information on careers in the food industry on www.careerschoices.org.uk

Retail assistant

There are no formal qualifications needed to work as a retail assistant, although most companies may ask for GCSEs/ Scottish Standard grades A–C/1–3, while some companies will require at least some A-levels. Apprenticeships are available for young people wanting a career in retail, leading to an NVQ/SVQ Levels 2 or 3. Also, NVQs/SVQs are available from Level 1 to 4 in Retail Operations.

Department or store manager

Entry to company management training programmes is open to those applicants who are aged over 18. Academic requirements are usually a minimum of A-levels/Higher grades or an equivalent qualification. Training takes between 18 months and two years. It often includes periods of training in a College or company training centre where you study for qualifications in business and customer services work.

Visual merchandiser

It is possible to move into visual merchandising after working as a retail assistant and helping with displays. No academic qualifications are required. NVQs/SVQs are available in Interior or Exhibition Design at Levels 2–4. However, many people do start with a full-time college course, leading to British Display Society (BDS) qualifications:

• General Certificate in Display – a one-year full-time course
• Technician Certificate – a one year part-time intensive study course.

Neither course requires any particular entry qualifications. Several colleges offer full-time courses such as the BTEC National Diploma in Design.

Finding a job

It is always best to first approach the company that you wish to work for; retail firms advertise vacancies within stores and on their websites, as well as in local newspapers. Alternatively, speak to your Connexions/careers service to get information about local Apprenticeships. Alternatively, you can contact the Retail Careerline freephone on 0800 093 5001.

CASE STUDY

John Coxon – Call Centre Customer Services Adviser, Virgin Mobile, Trowbridge

Sometimes, young people fall into jobs that they can do and yet which bring them little satisfaction apart from the wage at the end of the week. John had hoped to do an English degree and studied three A-levels, but was quite ill during Year 13 and failed to obtain the necessary grades. Unable to gain a place through Clearing, he decided to take a job and get on with life. Without advice and only a minimum of forethought, John signed up for shift work in the biggest call centre in town.

'I sit in a vast room with 30 or 50 other advisers. We all have headphones with attached microphones and our job is to take orders and answer queries about Virgin mobile phones. The callers can be frustrated from waiting to speak to a customer services adviser and occasionally they take it out on me – the voice at the end of the line. I always speak politely and try to defuse overheated situations.

'It's important to clockwatch or I can miss my break because a caller has particular problems with their mobile service. I have learned strategies that help to bring conversations to more speedy conclusions and, with greater knowledge, can now answer a much wider range of queries. At the start, I had to get a lot of help from my line manager.

'This job has opened my eyes to the behaviours and attitudes of the buying public and has confirmed my wish to help people with problems. I realise that often they have other issues which make their personalities appear difficult to handle.

'So, though I started this job as a fill-in, and I could train to become a supervisor next month, working towards NVQs at Level 2 and 3 in Customer Services, increased pay and more responsible work, I am actually starting a new job for a government service where I'll be answering the phone to young people who need advice and help. It's still shift work and I'm really just a 'listening ear', but I wish someone had advised *me* late at night! I'm looking forward to a new level of working where I'll gain qualifications in advice and guidance.'

USEFUL ADDRESSES

British Display Society
12 Cliff Avenue, Chalkwell
Leigh-on-Sea SS9 1HF
Tel: 020 8856 2030
www.britishdisplaysociety.co.uk

Customer Services
Customer Services Industry Authority
Oxford House
Sixth Avenue, Sky Business Park
Robin Hood Airport
Doncaster DN9 3GG
Tel: 08452 306080
www.habia.org.uk

Institute of Customer Service
2 Castle Court
St Peter's Street
Colchester CO1 1EW
Tel: 01206 571716
www.instituteofcustomerservice.com

Retail Advice Line: 0800 093 5001

Skillsmart Retail Ltd
The Sector Skills Council for Retail
4th Floor, 93 Newman Street
London W1T 3EZ
Tel: 020 7462 5060
www.skillsmartretail.com

13 Science, Maths and Statistics

SCIENCE

Scientific work is all about applying knowledge and logical thought to analyse problems, for example developing new technological solutions to providing alternative forms of energy. Scientists work by making predictions, then carrying out experiments to test those hypotheses, to see whether they were right or wrong. People working in science today are involved in finding ways to reduce greenhouse gas emissions, finding cures for diseases and sustainable sources of food, usually working to make the world a safer, more pleasant place.

Job opportunities

Science technicians work in hospital and industry labs and workshops under the direction of scientists. They check, operate and maintain equipment, prepare chemical solutions, collect samples, prepare specimens, perform experiments, collect results, analyse data and present their findings. They usually specialise in one particular area of science, such as: energy technology, nutrition, biochemistry, microbiology, pharmacology, satellite technology.

Skills and qualities

Anyone working in science needs to be interested in problem solving and must be good with their hands and able to think logically. They need a keen eye for detail, patience and determination, and the ability to work methodically and accurately. It is important to handle equipment deftly and to have good communication skills, both spoken and written. The work always involves being part of a team, so scientists have to work well with others.

Salaries

Rates of pay vary enormously with different companies and in different areas. A trainee technician's salary is likely to start at around £12,000, rising to £15,500 per annum with vocational qualifications and experience. The figure rises to around £18,000 for those with the equivalent of a degree; those technicians in management positions can earn considerably more – up to £40,000 annually.

Prospects

There are good opportunities for technicians, many of whom work for large organisations where there are openings into management positions and for specialisation.

Major employers

These include research companies, government departments, universities, hospitals, public health laboratories, and gas and electricity companies. All secondary schools, tertiary and further education colleges employ technicians in their laboratories.

Ways into work

Employers usually ask for a minimum of four GCSEs /Scottish Standard grades A–C/1–3 in English, maths and double science for technician posts. Laboratory assistant posts that involve rather more routine work may take those with fewer qualifications. These roles may accept applicants with a good general education where individuals also have practical skills.

One way into a career in science is through an Apprenticeship (see Introduction) leading to an NVQ/SVQ Level 2. This entry route is offered in:

- Food and drinks manufacturing operations
- Glass industry
- Health and social care
- Surface coatings industry

- Steel industry
- Water industry
- Optical manufacturing technology.

Advanced Apprenticeships leading to NVQ Level 3 can be obtained in all the above sectors of work, plus:

- Biotechnology
- Carpet manufacture
- Chemical sector firms
- Cosmetics industry
- Engineering maintenance or laboratory operations
- Gas industry
- Synthetic fibres
- Paper manufacturing
- Polymers
- Optical manufacturing technology
- Pharmacy technology
- Laboratory technology in education.

Apprenticeships in other scientific areas are being developed, offering NVQs/SVQs from Levels 1 to 5.

Specialist Diplomas in Health and Social Care are offered by schools and colleges for 14–19 year olds, from September 2008.

There are single and double award A-levels in Applied Science which provide an excellent basis for vocational work in science technology. Applied Science A-level – takes one or two years' study for students with GCSEs/Scottish Standard grades A–C/1–3.

BTEC/SQA National Diploma, Higher National Diploma and Higher National Certificate are also available in science subjects.

The professional body for science technicians is the Institute of Science Technology. It has its own qualifications: the Ordinary Diploma and Certificate and the Higher Diploma. It also offers its own vocational qualifications at preliminary and core levels through a number of registered centres.

Affiliate membership is open to anyone working or studying in science technology at NVQ/SVQ Level 1, at the Institute's Preliminary Vocational level (see below) or for an equivalent qualification.

Associate membership is open to those who hold an NVQ/SVQ Level 2 or have the Institute's Core Vocational Qualification.

Membership is awarded to applicants with an approved qualification such as NVQ/SVQ Level 3, a degree, HNC or HND.

Finding a job

For information about Apprenticeships contact the local Connexions/careers service or the Science, Technology and Mathematics Council (see Useful addresses). The Connexions service holds information about job opportunities for young work entrants.

If you're an adult with few formal qualifications, a one-year Access to Science course at an FE college can lead to a Foundation degree in Science and open an exciting career in the sciences, for example in the field of nutrition or nutritional therapy.

MATHS AND STATISTICS

For people who are a whiz with numbers, there are opportunities in all sectors of work and at every level of employment. Of course, the most responsible positions with the highest salaries are only open to degree-level maths graduates who may have specialised in statistics, but accuracy, speed and confidence with number work is vital in many job areas.

Job opportunities

Many organisations and businesses have their own market research, accounting and payroll departments, for example central and local government departments employ accounting clerks and statisticians to analyse survey data. Chapter 1 describes opportunities and entry qualifications for financial work in banks and building societies. Life assurance, actuary firms, pension companies and general insurance businesses all need numerate employees. Law firms employ law costs draughtsmen to calculate precise total costs of individual cases where different professionals have been engaged on a number of different tasks.

Skills and qualities needed

People who can work do rapid mental arithmetic – working out percentages, ratios, fractions and costs – can start work as quantity surveyors in the construction industry.

Others may prefer to work in the entertainment sector and are happy to be bingo callers or work in betting shops or for the Tote, or on cruise liners and in casinos as croupiers.

These jobs, and those where you working with or for the public, require customer service skills. You need good listening and negotiating skills and the ability to be firm yet friendly with awkward customers. For a number of jobs where you work with the public, you need to be highly presentable with a pleasant, sociable manner, whether in a work or leisure setting.

Salaries

Whether starting as a trainee accounts clerk or accounting technician, a bank officer or croupier, your salary will be around £10,000 per annum, but as you gain experience and qualifications in the work, your salary could reach £20,000+. With responsibilities and, possibly, results-related pay or commission, salaries can reach £40,000+.

Prospects

With maths and statistical ability, you will always be employable and could become a professional insurance broker, actuary, casino manager or law costs draughtsman, performing tricky calculations to arrive at the costs of lengthy court cases. Central and local government employ managers in their surveying, accounts and payroll departments.

Ways into the work

If you have a good pass in GCSE/Scottish Standard grade maths, or have obtained A-level/Higher grade maths then, with English language and a few other GCSEs/Scottish Standard grades at A–C/1–3, there are plenty of advertised opportunities. The Royal Statistical Society offers its own qualifications which are available to those with Level 2, 3 or 4 qualifications. Read the careers pages on its website (see Useful addresses below).

A specialised Diploma for 14–19 year olds in construction would be an excellent start for work as a quantity surveyor; from 2009, there will be a Diploma offered in Business administration and Finance.

Information about local Apprenticeships using maths skills can be obtained from your local Connexions/careers service, which also holds a list of local job opportunities. NVQs/SVQs at Levels 2 and 3 would be available in your specialist field of work – quantitative surveying, casino operations etc.

Finding a job

There are several websites which list vacancies at every entry level for those seeking jobs requiring ability with maths and/or stats. Scan the local newspapers as there are always positions for those with numeracy skills at Levels 2 and 3.

USEFUL ADDRESSES

Science

Institute of Science Technology
Kingfisher House
90 Rockingham Street
Sheffield S1 4EB
Tel: 0114 276 3197
www.istonline.org.uk

Institute: Science, Engineering and Technology
Courses/contacts: www.intute.ac.uk/sciences.html

Maths, statistics

Institute of Mathematics and Its Applications
Catherine Richards House
16 Nelson Street
Southend-on-Sea SS1 1EF
Tel: 01702 354200
www.ima.org.uk

Mathematical Association
259 London Road
Leicester LE2 3BE
Tel: 0116 221 0013
www.m-a.org.uk

Royal Statistical Society
12 Errol Street
London EC1Y 8LX
Tel: 020 7638 8998
www.rss.org.uk

PUBLICATIONS

Working in the Environment; Working in the Built Environment and Construction – 2006, VT Lifeskills, £8.50 each
Working in Law – 2005, downloadable from www.connexions-direct.com/winlaw

14 Security, Emergency and Armed Forces

This chapter covers a range of careers, from the Armed Forces – Army, Navy and RAF – to the work of the Police, Fire and Ambulance services. Today, there are many other areas where security guards or officers are deployed: civilian airports, prisons, remand centres, supermarkets, government buildings, hospitals, colleges and universities, but this work requires maturity, stamina and considerable experience with people of all kinds and is not suitable for young job entrants.

While each of the uniformed services has a long and proud tradition, today's operations use up-to-date technology and offer equal opportunities to young men and women from all backgrounds and ethnic groups.

AMBULANCE SERVICE

The majority of calls to the ambulance service are not 999 emergencies but pre-planned transfers of patients between hospitals, to outpatient appointments or home following inpatient treatment. The service is organised on a regional basis and recruitment and training vary from area to area.

Job opportunities

- Ambulance care assistant – driving and escorting routine non-emergency patients
- Ambulance technician – working with paramedics, answering urgent calls, travelling in ambulances, air ambulances or on motorcycles and administering pre-hospital treatment e.g. using ventilators to ease breathing difficulties
- Ambulance paramedic – doing similar work to a technician but additionally trained to administer drugs and treatments without a doctor's permission.

Skills and qualities needed

Ambulance personnel need to be warm and positive, and able to reassure injured and frightened people. They must be calm, be able to work as part of a team, have strong powers of concentration and good communication skills. Physical and emotional strength is important because the work can be distressing.

Salaries

A qualified ambulance care assistant earns around £12,000 annually. An ambulance technician earns around £17,500 while a paramedic earns around £20,000 per year.

Prospects

Care assistants can become technicians and then paramedics. Senior managers are usually promoted from the ranks. Most ambulance personnel work in the National Health Service, but there are some openings with private services.

Ways into work

Care assistant

You must be over 18 with a clean driving licence. Some services require a good standard of general education while others ask for four GCSEs/Scottish Standard grades A–C/1–3 in English and Maths. Scotland also requires a science subject. Training covers driving skills and emergency accident management and is followed by a probationary period at a station.

Technician

You need to be over 21 with a clean driving licence. Some services ask for a good standard of education while others are more specific. Scotland requires two A-levels/Highers. There is a national training programme for technicians, which includes emergency care, physiology and anatomy and advanced driving techniques. After training, technicians work under supervision for a year.

Paramedic

Paramedics can be chosen for training from technicians after a tough selection process. The training is demanding and includes time spent in a hospital operating theatre. Paramedics have to re-qualify every three years.

Finding a job

The Connexions/careers service gives advice on careers in the ambulance service. Information is also available from ambulance service headquarters, listed in the local phone directory.

CASE STUDY

Andrew Carr – Paramedic

Andrew is a paramedic team leader. As well as responding to urgent and emergency calls he is responsible for the administration of the ambulance station. This includes drawing up work rotas, recording absences and ordering equipment.

He is trained to give treatments including intubating patients, putting a plastic tube into the windpipe to clear airways, and inserting a cannula or tube into a vein through which drugs can be given. Drugs are given by paramedics for life-threatening situations such as cardiac arrest, seizures and diabetic comas.

Andrew took A-levels in Geography, Economics and Politics and went on to university.

In his words,

'It was a mistake. I was not very interested in my course. At the end of two years I decided to leave. I spent several years working in tourism in Portugal, before coming back to the UK and working with people with learning difficulties. I like caring for people, but I also like excitement, and that was what led me to apply to become a paramedic.

'There are several different pathways for paramedics, which vary slightly from area to area. I worked as a student ambulance technician for a year, then spent a year as a qualified technician before applying to become a paramedic.

'The work falls into two areas: urgent and emergency. Urgent calls are from doctors requesting that patients be taken to hospital within a set time, which could be two or four hours. Emergency calls are 999 calls that need a very quick response. We deal with major traumas such as traffic accidents, so paramedics need a strong stomach. They also need to be emotionally strong to cope with some depressing situations. The job can be dangerous, especially on Friday and Saturday nights when people are out drinking.

'All paramedics have to drive ambulances and pass an advanced driving course. Most importantly they also have to relate to people in any situation.

'I've been doing the job for 13 years and still find it exciting. There's the satisfaction of helping people and knowing that my high level of training means that I can make a difference between life and death.'

BRITISH ARMY

The Army plays an important role at home and abroad, taking part in humanitarian and peacekeeping assignments and carrying out a wide range of essential duties in war.

Job opportunities

The Army is divided into two parts:

- The Arms – made up of Combat Arms, the mainline fighting forces, and Combat Support Arms, which operate and fight in support of the Combat troops.
- The Services – which provide technical and administrative assistance.

Within the Arms and Services there are job opportunities in nine areas:

- Combat
- Engineering
- Further education
- Healthcare
- HR/administration and finance

- IT/communication
- Logistics
- Officer
- Specialist.

Skills and qualities needed

The Army prides itself on training recruits from different backgrounds to work together as a team. Soldiers need to be physically fit, keen to learn and eager to be part of a team.

Salaries

The most junior soldier receives £12,572 annually. This increases with time served and promotion. There is a pay review every year. For up-to-date information on rates of pay for all ranks see the Army website www.armyjobs.co.uk

Prospects

Promotion is based on individual merit rather than length of service. Promotion can be rapid and soldiers with strong leadership potential have the option to train as commissioned officers.

Ways into work

There are two main routes into the Army.

Single entry

This gives trainees aged between 16 years 9 months and 27 years direct access to over 100 different jobs, suiting a wide range of abilities. Some jobs are available to trainees up to age 33.

Junior entry

Army Foundation College

The college offers a one-year training programme for young people aged between 16 and 17 years 1 month who want to join the Army.

Army Development Course

This is a 17-week practical course at the Army Training Regiment at Bassingbourn for young people aged between 16 and 17 years 1 month who want to join the Army.

School Leavers' Scheme

The scheme is a 32-week practical course for trainees aged 16 years 9 months.

Army training leads to NVQs/SVQs, BTEC and City & Guilds qualifications. There are also opportunities to take GCSEs, A-levels and, for those who wish, a degree.

Finding a job

Full details of opportunities are available from local Armed Forces Careers Offices, listed under 'Army' in your local phone directory. Also, have a look at the Army's careers website for teenagers at www.camouflage.mod.uk

FIRE SERVICE

Only one in five calls to the fire service is for help with a fire. The service also assists at road, rail and air traffic accidents, chemical spillages and floods, and educates the public in fire safety. There are 58 different fire brigades in England and Wales and eight in Scotland.

Job opportunities

There are three types of firefighter: wholetime, retained and volunteer. This section deals only with wholetime firefighters. There are 34,300 wholetime firefighters in the UK and there are always more applicants than vacancies.

Skills and qualities needed

Firefighters need to get on with different types of people – even those who are confused and difficult – and must be able to work under pressure as part of a team. Firefighters are practical people, physically very fit, with good eyesight, able to cope with working shifts, and with dangerous situations.

Salaries

A firefighter aged 18 entering the service earns £19,918 per year and a firefighter aged 24 and over earns £26,548 annually.

Prospects

All entrants begin as firefighters. There are no special entry arrangements for people with particular qualifications and promotion is on merit.

Ways into work

Entrants must be at least 18 years old. A good standard of education is required and some brigades ask for specific GCSE passes. There is a national fitness test and medical examination. Good vision is essential.

Initial training lasts approximately three months and includes theory and practical work. Recruits then move to a fire station where they spend a two-year probationary period. Training continues throughout a firefighter's career.

Many colleges run BTEC First and National Diploma courses in Public Services (Uniformed) which give a good idea of the type of work involved in the fire service, but do not guarantee a place in the fire brigade.

Finding a job

The Connexions/careers service gives advice on careers in the fire service. Information is also available from recruitment departments of local fire services, listed in the phone directory.

POLICE FORCE

Police work is not the exciting stream of bank robberies, abductions and murder hunts it appears to be on television.

However, for the right person it is an interesting and rewarding career. There are 43 local Police Forces in England and Wales and eight in Scotland. Between them they deal with more than 6 million 999 calls a year.

Job opportunities

Three-quarters of the UK's 140,000 police officers are constables, dealing with the public, carrying out patrols and coping with disturbances. To become a sergeant, a constable must pass the Sergeants' Exam. There are then opportunities for promotion and for specialisation in areas such as CID or Special Branch.

Skills and qualities needed

Police officers need to be physically and mentally fit. They have to cope with rude and aggressive behaviour. The shift system means disturbed sleep patterns and difficulties having a social life outside the Force. A sense of humour, strong observation skills, a good memory, communication skills and a desire to help people are essential.

Salaries

The starting pay for a police officer is £21,000, with pay increases at regular intervals. Five years after completion of initial training a police officer earns around £31,000 annually.

Prospects

Every year around 60,000 people apply to join the police and only 6,000 are accepted. New recruits spend two years as a probationary constable, working on the beat and spending time studying at one of six national police training centres. At constable level, there are good opportunities to specialise and to develop an interesting career. Officers who pass the Sergeants' Exam can aim for promotion up the ranks.

Ways into work

There are no set academic requirements for becoming a police officer, although candidates must show they have a good grounding in Maths and English by passing the Police Initial Recruitment Test.

Everyone goes through the same selection process. Applicants must be over 18 years and 6 months, be physically fit and have good eyesight. They also need either a clean driving licence or to be learning to drive. During selection they must show themselves to be determined, honest and enthusiastic. Rather than looking for a particular type, the Police Force wants interesting people who have done something with their free time, whether it is community service, self-defence or learning a foreign language.

Many colleges run BTEC First and National Diploma courses in Public Services (Uniformed). These give a good idea of the type of work involved and whether a person is suited to the Police Force, but they do not guarantee the offer of a job.

Finding a job

The Connexions/careers service gives advice on careers in the police. Information is also available from the headquarters of each Police Force, listed in local phone directories.

ROYAL AIR FORCE

The RAF was formed in 1918 when the Royal Flying Corps was joined with the Royal Naval Air Service. Today, it has a force of over 50,000 men and women employed in approximately 70 disciplines. There are three levels of entry into the RAF: commissioned officer, non-commissioned aircrew and airman/airwoman.

Job opportunities

Officer specialisms include pilot, weapon systems officer (navigator), air traffic controller, fighter controller, engineer, supply and administration, as well as specialists such as doctors, dentists, legal officers and chaplains.

All non-commissioned aircrew enter as weapon systems operators. Linguists are pre-streamed but all others are allocated to the specialisations of air loadmaster, acoustics or electronic warfare during their training.

Airmen/airwomen trades are many and varied (about 40 in total), from technicians to caterers, photographers to flight operations assistants and nurses to musicians.

Skills and qualities needed

All RAF personnel must be physically fit, motivated, good communicators and be able to work as part of a team – contributing their different skills under pressure. Officers must have leadership qualities, accept responsibility and be capable of motivating different types of people in diverse situations.

Salaries

On completion of initial training, normally an officer will earn £22,650 annually. On the award of their flying brevet, non-commissioned aircrew earn around £27,500 and airmen/airwomen earn a minimum of £15,677 after one year's service.

Prospects

The number of vacancies varies according to branch or trade. Promotion is awarded on individual performance against establishment vacancies. Commissions to officer status are available to all non-commissioned personnel who gain the required academic qualifications and have the right leadership qualities.

Ways into work

Basic officer entry requirements are two A-levels/Scottish Higher grades plus at least five GCSEs/Scottish Standard grades A–C/1–3, including English language and Maths. Equivalent qualifications may be acceptable. Selections are made at the

Officers and Aircrew Selection Centre (OASC) at the RAF College at Cranwell in Lincolnshire.

Entry as NCO aircrew usually requires five GCSEs/Scottish Standard grades A–C/1–3, including English Language and Maths. The specialisation dictates what other qualifications are needed. As for officers, selections are made at OASC.

Many airmen/airwomen jobs require no formal qualifications, while others require specific subjects and grades. Every candidate has to pass aptitude tests and a medical at an Armed Forces Careers Office.

Finding a job

The Connexions/careers service gives advice on careers in the RAF. Detailed information is available from Armed Forces Careers Offices (under Royal Air Force in the local phone directory) and on www.raf.mod.uk/careers/

CASE STUDY

Ben Hardy

Aged 29, Ben is a physical training instructor and a corporal in the RAF. He joined in 1996.

The RAF comprises training units and strike units. Working in a training unit, Ben's role is similar to that of a school PE teacher. A strike unit is made up of fully trained personnel and here the role of fitness instructors is to ensure personnel are fit for operations. They set up remedial packages where necessary and organise adventurous training such as rock climbing and hill walking.

After GCSEs, Ben took a two-year BTEC National course in Public Services at West Anglia College, King's Lynn, and was accepted for training with the Royal Marines.

He says,

'After a few months I began to feel I wanted to train for a craft that would give me a future other than being a soldier. A college friend had joined the RAF to train as a physical training instructor and, the more I spoke to him, the more I was drawn to the idea.'

Ben left the Marines and applied to the RAF, filling in the 'gap' year with casual jobs. More than ten years on, he has no regrets:

'It's a fantastic life. Since joining, I've gained military and civilian instructor qualifications in rock climbing, kayaking, skiing and in summer mountain leadership. The great things about the RAF are the cross-section of people you meet and the responsibility you're given from the very start. If you have a good idea, people really want to hear about it.'

ROYAL NAVY

The history of the Royal Navy dates back as far as 882, when King Alfred took part in a seaborne engagement in the Stour estuary that earned him the name 'Father of the Navy'. Today's Royal Navy is admired across the globe as a world leader.

Job opportunities

The Royal Navy is made up of four Fighting Arms:

- Amphibious – this includes the Royal Marines and the amphibious task group RN vessels.
- Surface Ships – maintain and operate all surface vessels.
- Fleet Air Arm – maintain and operate all fixed wing and rotary aircraft.
- Submarine Service – maintain and operate all submarines including the national Strategic Nuclear Deterrent.

Within these four Fighting Arms there are several Branches (or jobs) that can be grouped together as:

- Warfare – tactical use of weapons systems and operation of ships and submarines.
- Engineering – maintenance and operation of propulsion and generation machinery, including weapons systems.
- Supply – logistical and hotel services support.
- Medical – includes medical, dentistry and Queen Alexandra's Royal Naval Nursing Service (QARNNS).

- Fleet Air Arm – aircraft handlers and safety equipment specialists, all of whom are trained for emergency situations.
- Submarine – maintain, operate and provide logistical support to the submarine fleet.

SKILLS AND QUALITIES NEEDED

Naval personnel need to be team players, able to get on with others in a confined environment. They need to be very fit, self-disciplined, yet ready to obey orders. Officers must be good communicators, quick-thinking decision makers with strong leadership skills.

Salaries

Basic pay on entry for a non-technician is £12,572 per annum, rising rapidly after initial training to £15,677.

Prospects

Entry into the Navy is as an officer or a rating. All entrants go through basic training before beginning specialist training. There is a structured promotion system. A number of naval officers began their career as ratings.

Ways into work

Minimum entry requirements for Royal Navy and Royal Marines officers are two A-levels/Scottish Higher grades plus at least five GCSEs/Scottish Standard grades A–C/1–3, including English and Maths or the equivalent, such as a BTEC/SQA National qualification.

Officer entrants to QARNNS need a nursing qualification and two years' experience. You can apply for a commission after two years in the service.

Royal Navy candidates have to pass a fitness test, a selection test, an interview and a medical examination. Some trades also ask for specific qualifications.

Royal Marines must have a minimum height of 1.63 metres and have to pass a three-day course comprising written tests, physical exercises and an interview.

Finding a job

The Connexions/careers service gives advice on careers in the Royal Navy. Information on all available job opportunities is available from Armed Services Careers Offices, or from Officer Careers Liaison Offices for officers' jobs, listed in local phone directories and on the Royal Navy website www.royalnavy.mod.uk

USEFUL ADDRESSES

Ambulance Service Association (ASA)
Capital Tower
91 Waterloo Road
London SE1 8RT
Tel: 020 7928 9620
www.asa.uk.net

Other useful websites

The Army website: www.camouflage.mod.uk
Fire service website: www.fireservice.co.uk
Police Force Recruitment: www.police-information.co.uk
Royal Air Force website: www.raf.mod.uk/careers/
Royal Navy website: www.royal-navy.mod.uk

PUBLICATIONS

Real Life Guide: The Armed Forces – 2004, Trotman, £9.99
Real Life Guide: The Police Force – 2006, Trotman, £9.99
Working in Security – 2006, DfES, downloadable from www.connexions-direct.com/winsecurity

15 Transport

An efficient transport system, whether by land, sea or air, is essential to the success of many businesses. However expedient a production process may be, a company must be able to deliver goods promptly if it is to prosper.

Many products, including perishable items such as food and flowers, are traded internationally, so efficient transport systems are needed. Although there is a drive to obtain raw materials and food from locations close to home markets to reduce greenhouse gas emissions and despoiling of natural habitats for cash crops, there remains tremendous demand for cargo and passenger transport.

AIR

The aviation industry employs hundreds of thousands of people across the UK and transports passengers and freight to all parts of the world.

Job opportunities

- Airline pilots – flying aircraft on long and short haul flights
- Air cabin crew – looking after passengers
- Air maintenance engineers – inspecting, servicing and repairing aircraft
- Air traffic controllers (ATCO) – ensuring the 7000 aircraft that fly through UK airspace daily take off, travel and land safely.

Almost all jobs in the industry involve shift and weekend work.

Skills and qualities needed

Airline pilots

Pilots need to be practical, confident and level headed, able to remain calm under pressure. Pilots need powers of concentration and good communication skills, the ability to understand complicated technical material and to make mathematical calculations. Normal colour vision, excellent eyesight, motor skills and good hearing are essential.

Air cabin crew

The crew work with many different people, some of whom are nervous of flying, so they have to be reassuring and polite in all circumstances. They need to be able to stay calm in emergencies and be physically fit. It is important to have excellent communication skills and to work cheerfully as part of a team.

Aircraft maintenance engineers

These engineers must work accurately and efficiently at all times, even when under pressure to finish a job quickly. They need to have strong practical skills and be able to understand and follow manuals and drawings. Teamwork is important.

Air traffic controllers

A calm head is vital, and so is the ability to concentrate completely on the job. Controllers work as part of a team but also have to make decisions themselves. They need strong technical skills to understand complicated radar and computer systems and good communication skills to give clearly understood directions. Normal colour vision, good eyesight and hearing are essential.

Salaries

Rates of pay vary with different airlines and the type of aircraft being flown. A captain who is in overall charge of the plane is likely to earn between £40,000 and £75,000 annually. A first officer or co-pilot earns from £20,000 to £40,000.

Air cabin crew's basic starting salary is likely to be around £10,500 per year. Perks that add to this income are flight allowances and commission for in-flight sales. British Airways cabin crew earn up to £12,000 in their first year. All salaries increase with experience.

Air maintenance engineers without licences earn up to £15,000. The basic salary for licensed technicians can rise to £30,000 depending on the airport. These figures can be increased by shift allowances.

Trainee Air Traffic Controllers (ATCOs) start at £10,000 but after they become qualified Air Traffic Controllers earn £39,000 per annum, depending on their unit. This figure can rise to a salary of £85,000 for experienced ATCOs in highly responsible positions.

Prospects

Promotion for airline pilots is from first officer to captain and depends on having the right qualities and experience (flying hours and ratings) and on vacancies arising. It usually takes between seven and ten years to reach the position of captain.

There are opportunities for cabin crew to become cabin service managers, senior cabin attendants or pursers, or to transfer to ground administration duties.

Aircraft maintenance engineers can become senior engineers and move into supervisory posts or management positions.

Air traffic controllers progress through three grades – ATCO 3, to ATCO 2 and then to ATCO 1, which is a management grade.

Ways into work

Airline pilot

There are three types of flying licence:

- Private Pilot's Licence (PPL)
- Commercial Pilot's Licence (CPL)
- Airline Transport Pilot's Licence (ATPL).

An ATPL is needed to captain a commercial multi-pilot passenger plane, a 'frozen' ATPL being sufficient qualification for the co-pilot (see below). An ATPL can be gained through a private training school, at a cost of up to £70,000. Potential trainees have to pass an assessment programme and usually require a minimum of five GCSEs/Scottish Standard grades A–C/1–3 including English, Maths and Science for entry. Some schools may require AS or A-level/Higher grades.

Commercial airlines only very infrequently offer sponsorship for trainee airline pilots. Academic requirements are the same as for private training schools, plus two A-levels or Higher grades, preferably including Maths and Physics, or equivalent qualifications in science or engineering. Entry age is usually between 18 and 28.

Pilots with 150 hours' flying experience who trained with the Armed Forces or other organisations can train through a modular route. This involves attendance at a training school to cover the necessary theory. It takes around 26 weeks and costs a minimum of £20,000.

Training takes place at private training schools and normally lasts between 40 and 70 weeks. It includes both theory and practice. Course completers obtain a Commercial Pilot's Licence and a 'frozen' ATPL. This enables them to work as a first officer or co-pilot under the command of a captain. After they have gained 1,500 hours' flying experience, including specified night, cross-country and instrument flying, hold an Instrument Rating and multi-crew rating with a minimum of 500 hours as a pilot on multi-pilot aeroplanes under Instrument Flight Rules (IFR), they are awarded the ATPL.

Air cabin crew

Entry requirements vary. Some airlines want applicants to be educated to GCSE standard and others require four or five GCSEs/Scottish Standard grades A–C/1–3 including Maths and English, or equivalent qualifications. The minimum age is usually 19–21 and applicants must be of an acceptable weight in proportion to their height. Some airlines specify full colour vision and a minimum height requirement of 1.6 metres.

Knowledge of a second language is helpful, and essential for work with British Airways. Many airlines prefer their cabin crew to have experience of work in areas such as catering, retail or nursing. First aid qualifications are useful and so is the ability to swim, and a life-saving certificate.

Airlines have their own schools where training can take between four and six weeks and includes customs and immigration, passenger care, first aid, food and drink service and sales training. Some colleges offer courses leading to the Air Cabin Crew Intermediate Vocational Qualification. NB: Short courses that last only one or two days cannot offer this qualification and should be avoided.

Air maintenance engineer

Apprenticeships (see Introduction) are offered by some major airlines and independent aircraft maintenance organisations, which set their own entry requirements. Many ask for GCSEs/ Scottish Standard grades A–C/1–3 including English, Maths, Physics or Double Science, or equivalent qualifications.

Full-time college courses, which can lead to a career as an air maintenance engineer, are:

- City & Guilds 2590 Aeronautical Engineering Competencies course. Some colleges ask simply for science and maths ability, others for specific GCSE/Scottish Standard grades. This is a two-year, full-time course and provides the knowledge required to gain an NVQ/SVQ Level 3.
- SQA National Certificate in Aeronautical Engineering, which requires GCSE/Scottish Standard passes at A–C /1–3 in English, Maths and Science or Design Technology. This is offered at Perth College and lasts one year.
- BTEC National Diploma in Engineering (Aerospace Engineering, Maintenance Engineering or Aerospace Studies). This usually requires four GCSEs/Scottish Standard grades at A–C/1–3 in English, Maths and Science (to include Physics) or an equivalent qualification. It is offered at several colleges – also through training in the RAF – and is open to students and employees sponsored by airline companies.

Training is linked to the licensing system, which enables engineers to check and certify their own work and that of other people. The common European aircraft maintenance licence is known as Joint Aviation Requirement (JAR) 66. To gain JAR 66, engineers must complete a basic training course or an exam and gain relevant work experience. Only full-time Civil Aviation Authority (CAA) courses lead to the full JAR 66 licence.

Air traffic controller

Most ATCOs are employed by National Air Traffic Services Ltd (NATS) and work at area control centres, controlling planes in the sky. Others work at airports and deal with planes taking off and landing.

Applicants need to be between ages 18 and 27, with GCSE/Scottish Standard grades A–C/1–3, plus A-level or Higher grades or an equivalent qualification. They have to pass two selection stages.

NATS initial training lasts 74 weeks at the College of Air Traffic Control near Bournemouth and varies according to the type of work trainees will be doing: working at area control centres or at airports. After the initial training period students are posted to a unit to qualify as an ATCO through practical training and work towards a Certificate of Competency.

Finding a job

For information about Apprenticeships contact your local Connexions/careers service which also has information about work-based training opportunities.

Sponsored pilot-training places have now ceased, however the Cabair Group of Aviation Companies (see under Useful addresses) occasionally lists airlines that are willing to sponsor worthwhile students.

Numbers of air cabin crew are increasing. Some are employed by airlines that fly around the world, while others operate on a Europe-wide, even UK-wide, basis. Anyone interested in air cabin crew work should contact specific airlines directly.

Only large aviation companies run engineer training programmes, while smaller companies recruit trained aircraft maintenance engineers. Competition for places is strong, but there is considerable demand for trained engineers.

At present NATS is recruiting large numbers of trainee ATCOs each year (see Useful addresses).

LAND

Rail

Until 1994 the rail industry was a single, government-owned company. Today there are 200 rail companies responsible for both running and maintaining passenger train services across the country. Network Rail manages and maintains the track and operations and there are freight-operating companies which train manufacturers and maintainers in rail support operations. Over 150,000 people work in the rail industry and, at present, there are around 5,000 vacancies across all jobs and professions.

Job opportunities

Rail opportunities include:

On-board staff

- Train driver/shunter
- Catering staff
- Guard
- Ticket inspector.

Operations/station staff

- Control room operator
- Station platform staff
- Ticketing staff
- Signaller
- Finance
- Human resources
- Information technology team
- Planning and scheduling
- Sales staff
- Cleaners
- Station catering staff.

Rolling stock, track development and maintenance staff

- Track engineer
- On-track plant operator
- Signal and telecoms engineer

- Civil engineer
- Electrification engineer
- Rolling stock engineer.

Skills and qualities needed

Everyone working in the rail industry needs a very high awareness of safety issues. Concentration at all times is vital, even when the work is routine. Staff dealing with the public have to be patient and courteous and need good communication skills.

Salaries

Salaries vary widely, for example trained ticketing staff can earn from £10,000 up to £18,500 annually. Drivers with experience earn from £25,000 to £40,000 a year.

Ways into work

Apprenticeships (see Introduction) leading to NVQs/SVQs at Levels 2 or 3 are available in Rail Engineering and in Rail Operations.

Although 18 is the minimum age to train as a train driver on London Underground, many companies operating on the main network will not consider applicants under 21. Safety is a vital issue, strict regulations apply and drivers have to undergo regular assessments throughout their career. Some train operating companies carry out driver training themselves, while others put it in the hands of specialist training providers. Qualifications for drivers include NVQ/SVQ Level 2 in Rail Transport Operations (Driving) and a City & Guilds qualification in Process Engineering Maintenance.

Finding a job

For information about Apprenticeships contact your local Connexions/careers Service. Further information about careers in the rail industry is available on www.careersinrail.org or from the Centre for Rail Skills (see GoSkills in Useful addresses).

CASE STUDY

Colette Mulkeirins

Colette works for Network Rail – the rail maintenance company. She is part of a maintenance team responsible for checking signals, tracks, points and other equipment. Aged 22, she has worked in rail maintenance for five years.

After taking GCSEs, Colette followed the advice gained from a careers interview and thought about civil engineering as a career. She joined a training scheme run by the Construction Industry Training Board but was unable to find an employer to sponsor her course.

In Colette's words,

> 'At the time I was looking for sponsorship, I was offered a place on a pilot course run by the Railway Training Scheme, and decided to take it. I joined Network Rail and within six months was offered an Apprenticeship by the company. Since completing my Advanced Apprenticeship – gaining NVQ Level 3 in Railway Maintenance – I have done courses in signalling, powered plant and safety.
>
> 'My day usually runs from 7.00 am to 4.00 pm. As soon as I arrive I pick up a work sheet and join my team. There are usually five of us and we're briefed on the work we're to do before going out. Once we all know what we're doing, and how to carry out the work safely, we set off with our tools and equipment.
>
> 'I never wake up and feel miserable about having to go to work because I like it so much. Railways are always likely to be there, so I have job security. Working outside means you get used to the weather, and while I may be out in the rain when other people are inside, I'm out in the sun when they're stuck in an office.'

ROAD

Not only do many people rely on local and national bus services for travel, over 85% of goods are carried across the country by road haulage companies, varying in size from small companies with a single vehicle to organisations with a thousand-vehicle fleet. Today, 1.75 billion tonnes of freight is moved by heavy goods vehicles on UK roads each year; this volume will rise only minimally by 2010.

The type of driving licence required depends upon the sort of vehicle to be driven:

- Large Goods Vehicles (LGV) licence is required to drive vehicles above 3.5 tonnes.
- Category C1 licence is required to drive a vehicle between 3.5 and 7.5 tonnes.
- Category C licence is for vehicles over 7.5 tonnes.
- Category C+E licence for articulated vehicles.
- Passenger Carrying Vehicle (PCV) licence is required to drive a bus with more than nine passenger seats.

Job opportunities

These include delivery drivers and bus or coach drivers.

Skills and qualities needed

Work involves long periods on the road, so drivers need to enjoy driving, have good eyesight, excellent powers of concentration and be reasonably fit and healthy. They need good practical driving skills and the patience to deal with other drivers on the road. Bus drivers dealing with members of the public need tact and a friendly manner to get on well with all types of people.

Salaries

Drivers can earn between £12,000 and £18,000 per year, depending on the company and the type of vehicle driven.

Prospects

At present, there is a shortage of licensed lorry drivers across the UK. Stricter control of permitted weekly hours at work has meant that more drivers are required and companies are actively recruiting entrants. There is no set promotion ladder for drivers, but there are opportunities to move into supervisory or management posts.

Ways into work

No formal academic qualifications are needed to train as a driver. Some companies train their own drivers and put them through the appropriate test. It is also possible to train privately at a specialist driving school to gain both LGV and PCV licences.

Apprenticeships are available in two frameworks: Road Haulage and Distribution, and Driving Goods Vehicles, accredited by NVQs/SVQs are available at Levels 1–5.

Skills for Logistics, the Sector Skills Council for the road haulage and distribution industry, runs a Young LGV Driver Scheme that enables trainees under 20 to follow a fast-track programme to a Category C licence at age 18 and gain an NVQ/SVQ Level 2.

Finding a job

For information about Apprenticeships contact your local Connexions/careers service. Further information about the Young Driver Scheme is available from Skills for Logistics (see Useful addresses).

SEA

The Merchant Navy

Britain has a long maritime tradition and UK waters are some of the busiest in the world, with over 90% of trade arriving or leaving by sea. The Merchant Navy offers great opportunities for capable and enthusiastic young people to manage and operate modern, technically sophisticated ships.

Job opportunities

The British Merchant Fleet (Merchant Navy) consists of a large number of ships operated by individual shipping companies. It operates worldwide and includes:

- The world's largest and most modern ferry sector
- Some of the most prestigious cruise companies in the world

- Containerships carrying a variety of cargo
- High quality oil, gas and chemical tankers of all sizes
- Modern bulk carriers carrying ores, grain and coal
- Specialised vessels, including survey ships and those supporting the offshore exploration industry.

The master or captain is in charge of the entire ship. The ship's engineering and technical systems are the responsibility of the chief engineer. Deck officers control navigation, communications, cargo handling and ship stability. Working for these officers are deck ratings who have a lower level of responsibility. Engineer officers are responsible for all the technical services on board, while engineer ratings support them by carrying out routine maintenance and repairs.

There are some dual officer roles that cover both deck and engineering departments.

Catering and hospitality support services are required on cruise ships and passenger ferries, which are run on the lines of a large hotel. Specific roles vary between shipping companies and, generally, prior qualifications and experience in the catering, hotel or hospitality industry are necessary. There are jobs for pursers/receptionists, restaurant and bar staff, casino staff, housekeepers, cruise directors, entertainers, hairdressers, beauticians, photographers, child care and retail staff.

Skills and qualities needed

On board ship, work is divided into shifts or watches which are usually four hours on and eight hours off. Leave time is generous but the job means working unsocial hours with some long periods at sea, depending on the type of ship and its trading pattern. Merchant seamen need to take responsibility when necessary and respond quickly to any emergency. A sense of humour and tolerance are required to live in close contact with others. Good health and eyesight are essential.

Salaries

Pay depends on rank and the shipping company.

A rating earns between £16,000 and £21,000 a year, a junior officer earns between £17,000 and £21,000, a senior officer earns between £21,000 and £45,000. Officer cadets have tuition and course fees paid, plus a salary or training allowance of around £4,500 to £7,000.

Prospects

There are four main entry routes: Marine Traineeship, Marine Apprenticeship, Officer Cadet Training and Graduate Entry. Each provides promotion opportunities through to the ranks of master/captain or chief engineer.

Ways into work

Entry is at age 16, 18 or 21 and above. All the training programmes have alternating periods at college and at sea. Trainees are sponsored by their training company.

- Marine Traineeship Deck and Engineering – requires at least three GCSEs or Scottish Standard grades or equivalent qualification.
- Marine Apprenticeship Deck and Engineering – requires at least four GCSEs/Scottish Standard grades in English, Maths, Physics or Double Science, or equivalent qualification.
- Officer Cadet Training Deck and Engineering – requires at least four GCSEs/Scottish Standard grades A–C/1–3 in English, Maths, Physics or Double Science, together with A-levels/Scottish Highers or equivalent.

Finding a job

The Connexions/careers service gives advice on careers in the Merchant Navy. The first step is to gain sponsorship from a shipping company or training organisation. A full list of such companies offering deck, engineering and electro-technical cadetships is available from the Merchant Navy Training Board (details in Useful addresses) and on the Merchant Navy website: www.mntb.org.uk.

USEFUL ADDRESSES
Air

Association of Licensed Aircraft Engineers
Bourn House
8 Park Street
Bagshot GU19 5AQ
Tel: 01276 474888
www.alae.org

British Air Line Pilots Association
BALPA House
5 Heathrow Boulevard
278 Bath Road
West Drayton UB7 0DQ
Tel: 020 8476 4000
www.balpa.org.uk

The Cabair Group of Aviation Companies
Elstree Aerodrome
Borehamwood WD6 3AW
Tel: 020 8236 2400
www.cabair.com

Civil Aviation Authority
CAA House
45–59 Kingsway
London WC2B 6TE
Tel: 020 7379 7311
www.caa.co.uk

NATS – National Air Traffic Services
Corporate and Technical Office
4000 Parkway
Whiteley
Fareham PO15 7FL
Tel: 01489 616001
www.nats.co.uk

Royal Aeronautical Society
4 Hamilton Place
London W1J 7BQ
Tel: 020 7670 4300
www.raes.org.uk

Rail

GoSkills – Sector Council for Passenger Transport
Concorde House, Trinity Park
Solihull B37 7UQ
Tel: 0121 635 5520
www.goskills.org

Road

Skills for Logistics – Sector Skills Council for Moving,
Handling or Storing Goods
14 Warren Yard
Warren Farm Office Village
Stratford Road
Milton Keynes MK12 5NW
Tel: 01908 313360
www.skillsforlogistics.org

Sea

The Merchant Navy Training Board
Carthusian Court
12 Carthusian Street
London EC1M 6EZ
Tel: 020 7417 2800
www.mntb.org.uk
www.careersatsea.org

PUBLICATIONS

Working in Airports – 2005, DfES, downloadable
www.connexions-direct.com/winairports

Working in Transport and Logistics – 2006, VT Lifeskills,
£8.50

Real Life Guide: Passenger Transport – 2006, Trotman,
£9.99

Real Life Guide: Distribution and Logistics – 2006, Trotman,
£9.99